॥ S

The Drops of Nectar

(Amṛta-Bindu)

tvameva	mātā	ca	pitā	tvameva
tvameva	bandhuśca	sakhā		tvameva
tvameva	vidyā	draviṇaṁ		tvameva
tvameva	sarvaṁ	mama		devadeva

त्वमेव	माता	च	पिता	त्वमेव
त्वमेव	बन्धुश्च	सखा		त्वमेव।
त्वमेव	विद्या	द्रविणं		त्वमेव
त्वमेव	सर्वं	मम		देवदेव॥

Swami Ramsukhdas

Seventh Reprint   2009   3,000

Total   19,000

❖   **Price : Rs. 10**

(Ten Rupees only)

ISBN 81-293-0092-3

Printed & Published by :

Gita Press, Gorakhpur—273005 (INDIA)

(a unit of Gobind Bhavan-Karyalaya, Kolkata)

Phone - (0551) 2334721, 2331250; Fax - (0551) 2336997
e-mail : **booksales@gitapress.org** website : **www.gitapress.org**

[1407]

Foreword

For the relief of those afflicted by worldly suffering and others seeking guidance on the right path to eternal bliss, this book called the Amṛta-Bindu (The Drops of Nectar) is being offered. Its priceless selection has been made from the collections of the elixir-like discourses of Parama Shraddheya Swami Shri Ramsukhdasji Maharaj. For many years, these ethereal "drops" have appeared in and were published by the monthly magazine, 'Kalyana'. For the convenience of readers, these have been classified under different topics and are brought out in the form of a book, of the above name.

Verily, each drop embraces in itself a whole ocean of thought. Through simple words, special meanings are pregnant; reading is easy, without consuming much time and no effort is involved in digesting and understanding these maxims. Dealing with various subjects, the reflected essence is useful for all; who knows at what time and which maxim, might change the whole course of life of an individual, remove one's illusions and overcome his difficulties; and eliminate worry, grief and disquietude!

Brothers and sisters of all classes, therefore, should take advantage of this collection and by the shower of this nectar try to make their lives beautiful, happy and bountiful. What more could one wish! Humbly.

—*R. K. Dhawan*

|| Śrī Hariḥ ||

The Drops of Nectar
(Amṛta-Bindu)

While the rhythm and resonance of the expressions of Parama Shraddheya Swami Shri Ramsukhdasji Maharaj, is pleasing to the head and heart, it is difficult to translate the perfection of the Amṛta-Bindu maxims, compiled by Shri R. K. Dhawan, and communicate the same in precise English. However, a faithful effort has been made to capture the spiritual essence of the original Hindi selections. The result is presented in the hope that this book would be acceptable to the readers and it gives them as much pleasure and satisfaction, as it has given me to absorb and translate. Should the reader, however, notice any inadequacies or shortcomings, the fault lies entirely, with me and would be considered on reprinting.

—*R. N. Kaul*

CONTENTS

S. No. Topic		Page

The Drops of Nectar

(Amṛta-Bindu)

(I) Eternal Pleasure

In seeking pleasure for ourselves, we gain pleasure that perishes, and on making others happy, we enjoy perpetual pleasure. (1)

The heavens are for enjoying pleasure and the hell for pain. Rising above pleasure and pain, we can achieve bliss, in this human world. (2)

Whatever pleasure we gain by detachment from the world, could never be gained by our attachment to it. (3)

So long as we continue to seek perishable pleasure, till then, we cannot acquire perpetual bliss. (4)

The enjoyment of perishable pleasure turns stale and comes to an end; while God's everlasting pleasure, remains fresh and keeps increasing. (5)

(II) Pride

The pride of goodness, is the root of evil. (6)

By discarding selfishness and pride, one achieves saintliness. (7)

One's pride in intellect, prevents absorption of words of Śāstras and saints, into the inner faculty. (8)

Whatever is special about caste and class, is for the service of others, but not for pride.   (9)

As much pride you take in your goodness, so much more evil you would create. So do good and take no pride in it.   (10)

Knowledge leads to salvation, but its pride to hell.   (11)

In acquiring worldly objects, one could feel proud, but in attaining God pride never arises and is ever destroyed.   (12)

Without giving up selfishness and pride, man never achieves greatness.   (13)

Where there is pride of class, devotion is difficult, because devotion is through the self, not through the body. But class belongs to the body, and not to the self.   (14)

So long as one is selfish and proud, one could not love anybody.   (15)

A proud person serves less, but feels he serves much more. The humble feel it as less, but serve much more.   (16)

The vanity of wisdom, arises from foolishness. (17)

What is one's own, does not make one vain, and what is not own, also does not give vanity. Vanity comes from things that are not one's own, but are treated as own.   (18)

The vanity to assume full knowledge only for part,

makes one an atheist. Not content with what one knows and seeks more knowledge, makes him a seeker.   (19)

When a community, creed, ideology, scripture, person etc., stress upon renunciation of selfishness and vanity, they are great, but by exhorting these for self and pride, they become degenerate.   (20)

(III) Ego (I-ness)

I-ness, is the seed of the world.   (21)

Assuming the body as "I and mine", one gets a variety of endless pains.   (22)

By giving up ego, an endless creation is forsaken, as it is ego, that sustains the whole world.   (23)

"I am bound"— The "I" in it is the same as in "I am free," or "I am Brahma" also includes the "I". The removal of this "I", is in reality, liberation.   (24)

The world, the being and God, these three are one, but because of our ego appear separate.   (25)

In truth, detachment should be from the body. Segregation from society, does not eliminate ego or individuality, but strengthens it.   (26)

Our own self is divinely Eternal Existence, and it has no ego. If this is realized immediate salvation results.   (27)

Struggle does not come from caste or religion, but arises from selfishness and ego.   (28)

Seeing something special in oneself, means

strengthening of ego, finiteness and bodily pride. (29)

God's creation reflects the image of God, but the beings give it an image of the world by their ego, attachment and fondness.   (30)

(IV) Objective (Goal)

W orldly success or failure constitute no obstacle to a man who has made God-realization as the only objective of his life for which he is blessed with this human body.   (31)

Just as the goal of the sick, is to gain good health, so man's objective is to seek salvation. By giving no importance to worldly success or failures and remaining equanimous, man achieves his goal. (32)

When the sole objective of an aspirant is to realise God, then whatever resources, things, conditions etc., he has, all become God-oriented.   (33)

A firm determination to realise God as a goal, leads to quick purity of the inner faculty, compared with any other religious effort or ritual.   (34)

Even animals satisfy their senses, but such satisfaction is not the goal of man's life. His goal is to seek the Reality devoid of pain or pleasure.   (35)

Karmayoga, Jñānayoga, Dhyānayoga, Bhaktiyoga and other means, necessitate a firm determination and goal. Without a resolve for the goal, how could the means ensure salvation?   (36)

When the sole objective is to realise God, no means are small or great.   (37)

In reality, beyond God-realisation, man's objective is nothing else; the necessity is to recognise this objective and then to fulfil the same.   (38)

The objective of attaining Divinity is the glory of man but for such objective man does not deserve to be called a human being.   (39)

(V) Progress

If a thing or circumstance does not exist now, and to assume progress, success and smartness in achieving these, is a great error. Non-existing thing cannot exist forever—it is a rule. Whatever is perennial, remains so always, achieving such a thing (Godly essence) is in reality progress, success or smartness.   (40)

The achievers of spiritual success, automatically gain worldly progress.   (41)

Think—should we ourselves disregard our knowledge, so, how could we attain progress? (42)

True progress, in reality is, the purity of our tendencies of Nature.   (43)

Worldly progress is not a thing of the present, nor is spiritual advance one of the future.   (44)

One who seeks an easy life, could not really progress.   (45)

Just as a tree may rise high without limit, there is no limit to a man's ascent. (46)

In the spiritual path of man's progress, his attachment to pleasures born of contact is a special impediment. (47)

The rise and fall of man is through his sentiment and attitude but not by things, circumstances etc. (48)

Congruence of intellect and mind and concordance between mind and senses, facilitates progress. However, the subservience of mind to the senses and that of the intellect to the mind, leads to a fall. (49)

(VI) Solitude

True solitude arises from one's delinking of his body, senses, mind and intellect. (50)

One ought not to make his spiritual discipline dependant upon any circumstance, it may be solitude or company of men. One ought to make such discipline according to one's own circumstances. (51)

One desirous of solitude is dependent on circumstance; one who remains subject to such dependance is a seeker of pleasure but not an aspirant (Bhogī not a Yogī). (52)

An aspirant should have neither attraction for the public, nor for solitude. Circumstances do not bring about salvation rather it follows detachment. (53)

To go to unpeopled places or to lie alone, is

mistaken solitude, so long as the body of this world, the seed is there. So long as there is a link with the body, one continues to be attached to the world. (54)

The body is a part of the world. So detachment of the body and not to have any ego or mineness for the same, is true solitude. (55)

Interest in solitude for an aspirant is good, but not with any attachment. Insistence on solitude might cause disturbance in his inner faculties on not getting it and reinforce the importance of the world. (56)

(VII) Duty

M an could carry out his duties, under every circumstance. Service is the real emblem of duty. In other words, it means utilising worldly bestowed body and materials, for the benefit of the world. (57)

Man who carries out his duties, is naturally happy in his mind. As against this, failure to do one's duty makes man automatically depressed. (58)

An aspirant could be free of attachment, only if through his body, senses, mind and intellect, he recognises these as not "mine", nor "for me", but only of the world, for the world and for its good, only acts diligently and regularly to carry out his duties. (59)

In these times, in homes and in society, is seen much unhappiness, quarrels and confrontation. The basic reason is that, though people demand their rights, they do not discharge their own duties.   (60)

No act of duty, is by itself small or big. But selfless undertaking the smallest and the largest service equates these.   (61)

Acting for the good of others, that is duty. Any act that causes harm to anybody, is contrary to duty. (62)

Because of attachment or aversion, man has to strive or face difficulties, in carrying out his duties. (63)

What, one must do and can do, is called duty. Not doing one's duty is an error. Negligence of duty is stupid and leads to hell, **'Narakastama unnāho'** (Śrīmad Bhāgavata XI. XIX. 43).   (64)

Acts which bring pleasure to one's own self are called 'unreal', while those for the good of others, are termed 'real'. Unreal actions lead to births and deaths and real acts result in God-realization.   (65)

Do better and better acts, but not in the belief, that the world is permanent.   (66)

One acting without thought of reward, he alone, can readily discharge his duties.   (67)

Merely watching other's act, could never engross one in his duties, watching other's duties is undutiful.   (68)

Whether a family man or a monk (Sādhu), one who acts rightly according to his duties, he is great.   (69)

Selfish acts for oneself are contrary to duties (leading to bondage).   (70)

By following one's duties, one could become a dispassionate 'धर्म तें बिरति'—(Mānasa 3/16/1), but if one does not become so, then he has not fulfilled his duties, correctly. (71)

We know our duties, but desire and affection prevent us from deciding to carry these out. (72)

Among the four castes (Varṇas) and stages of life, it is the great who discharge their duties, and those who do not, remain small. (73)

All the worldly relations are for performing one's duties not to claim rights. One is to give pleasures to them not to seek pleasures from them. (74)

With the awareness of the goal of salvation (Kalyāṇa) one might learn his duties, even without the study of Śāstras. And without knowing his own objective, he would, despite study of the scriptures not become aware of his duties, on the contrary his ignorance would increase, this we know. (75)

(VIII) Benediction (Kalyāṇa)

I have nothing of my own, I want nothing, I have to do nothing for myself. These three ideas lead quickly to benediction. (76)

The resolve of God, is for our salvation. If we have no resolve of our own, then God's resolve automatically would lead to our liberation. (77)

There are no circumstances in the world, in which

the salvation of man could not be achieved, as God is equally present in all circumstances.   (78)

Attaining divinity is very easy, but if there is no desire for the same, of what use is that easiness? (79)

The work of the world could be undertaken by somebody else but who could look after one's emancipation except himself, just as food and medicines have to be taken by the person himself. (80)

No new circumstances are necessary for one's self-redemption. A proper use of existing circumstances could result in salvation.   (81)

Redemption does not result from action, but from feelings and discrimination.   (82)

If people living in a home, treat themselves as servants, and others as masters, then all will be served and it would lead to benediction for everybody. (83)

The love of pleasure leads to births and deaths, while the love of God, brings redemption.   (84)

Those desirous of good to self, if they pray to God in true faith, would be ushered into His presence and be heard and receive benediction soon.   (85)

If emancipation comes to a person, it should be either through blessings of a saint, or by God's grace.   (86)

There is no shortage in the world of saints, or preceptors, but in the interest of one's own redemption, a person must by his own devotion, intense desire, feelings and faith, help himself. (87)

(IX) Desire (Kāmanā)

S o long as an aspirant desires his own happiness, ease, respect and greatness etc., his individuality is not destroyed. And without that happening his separation from God continues.   (88)

Until after our inner faculty is completely free from desire, we do not need to aspire for God, as He would on His own, be realised.   (89)

Worldly desires initiate animal behaviour and with aspiration for God, humanity begins.   (90)

Desire is in, "meeting my mind's wish." It is desire that is the cause of sorrow and without renouncing desire, nobody can achieve real happiness.   (91)

How to gain happiness? Only in its pursuit, man fails in his duties and degrades himself.   (92)

With the birth of his desires, man turns away from his duty, his own self and God and comes face to face, with the perishable world.   (93)

Aspirants should neither hope to fulfil worldly desires, nor despair from lack of fulfilment, of godly aspiration.   (94)

For the renunciation of desire all are free, rightful, capable and competent, but in the satiation of desires, none is free, rightful, capable and adequate.   (95)

As desires are, steadily destroyed, so would

saintliness arise, accordingly. And if desires increase, so would piety vanish. The root of unrighteousness is desire itself.   (96)

From mere desire, one gets no material benefits and if one gets any, these never stay forever with him, even though it is apparent, desire for material things is a great error.   (97)

Life is harsh when allied people desire sensual happiness, death becomes a suffering, if man longs to live.   (98)

If the desire for matter gets satisfied, one has to make effort, and if the desire for life can be achieved, man would try to avoid death. But by desire alone neither one gets the things one wishes, nor is he saved from death.   (99)

All are free to renounce desire and are not dependent upon others. For satisfying desire, one is subservient upon others and none is free.   (100)

The desire for happiness, hope and enjoyment, these three are causes of all miseries.   (101)

By giving up liking for ephemeral things, one achieves the eternal truth.   (102)

One wills happenings this way or that way, such a dilemma means unhappiness.   (103)

To desire respect for ourselves, results in disrespect for us.   (104)

To be covetous for a thing in the mind, is wretchedness indeed. The desire for acquisition, always makes one indigent. (105)

The wish for the destructible, is by itself the impurity of our inner-faculty (intellect, instinct and ego). (106)

Man does not have to give up action, but only to renounce desire. (107)

Man is not enslaved by things, but by desire for them. (108)

Should you want peace, give up your desires. (109)

The desire for taking anything, leads to dreaded unhappiness. (110)

One who has desire within him, he somehow, becomes dependent on others. (111)

To seek happiness for oneself, is a demoniac and bedevilled propensity. (112)

Just as, one gets misery without seeking it, so one receives pleasure without desire. An aspirant should never desire for worldly happiness. (113)

Desire for enjoyment and hoarding, both only lead to sin and are of no use. So renounce this desire. (114)

The Desire for self-enjoyment and accumulation degrades man, to worse than animals. Abjuring of this desire, raises one, higher than even the divine (Devas). (115)

What things belong to us, we shall ever receive and none else could take these away. So without seeking anything, do your duty.   (116)

'As I desire, so it should be'—so long as we have such a wish, we cannot have peace.   (117)

Even though man may be sensible, yet surprisingly he desires things having a beginning and an end. This is strange.   (118)

In accepting one's existence through the body, man desires the perishable and because of this, his stake hardens.   (119)

By desire, one may or may not get something, but in giving up desires, he gets everything.   (120)

We do not like condemnation, as we want appreciation. We seek appreciation, because in reality, we are not fit for the same. For those who deserve it, they do not wish for it.   (121)

By desiring to seek appreciation from others, is a great weakness. Therefore, be good and not be called good.   (122)

To shun worldly pleasure would be necessary, sometime or the other; so why delay?   (123)

As far as possible, try to fulfil the hopes of others, but have no expectations from them.   (124)

Ponder, if from whom you seek happiness is he

himself quite happy? Is he not unhappy? How could an unhappy person make you happy? (125)

The happiness one gets by forsaking desire, could never be matched by satisfying desires. (126)

If you want fervent yearning for God, then give up craving for the world. (127)

One who desires the ever changing world, and draws happiness from it, he also changes and passes through the cycle of births and deaths. (128)

What we could not keep forever with us, what use is its desire or acquisition? (129)

The feelings of want are caused by desire and without desire, there could be no shortage. (130)

If we give up desires forever, then essential things would become available, automatically. Such things covet a person who has given up all desires. (131)

One who longs for things for his pleasure, has to face the agony of their want. (132)

One who has no desires within himself, his needs are met by nature (Prakṛti), on its own. (133)

What does not stay with us always, nor do we stay with that forever. To desire its acquisition or draw pleasure from it, is foolish and degrading. (134)

By desiring happiness, happiness is not granted. This is a rule. (135)

You may be a saint or remain a householder until

you seek desire, (and to acquire things) you will never gain peace.   (136)

If you want peace, give up "the desire for acquisition of this or that", "what God wishes that should come true", and welcome the same.   (137)

All acts done with desire are unreal, their fruit is perishable.   (138)

Seeking (desiring) anything is slavery, and not desiring it, is liberation.   (139)

For not getting things, we are not unfortunate. But even with being a fraction of God, to desire perishable things—is our misfortune.   (140)

By the desire of pleasure, duality arises, and without such desires, there is no duality.   (141)

So long as we accept our body as our own, then our desires would not be wiped out.   (142)

Reflect upon, that we remain the same, with or without fulfilment of our desires; then what did we gain by realisation of our wish and what loss we suffered, from its non-fulfilment? What differences did it make to us?   (143)

(X) Master and Disciple

One who becomes the Guru of the world, in fact turns into a slave of the world. One who becomes a master of his self, he becomes the master of the world.   (144)

For one's redemption, our own aspiration counts. If we are not keen, of what help could the Guru or the Śāstras be? (145)

If somebody wants anything from us, how could he be our Guru? (146)

To make a son or disciple greater than oneself, is a rule or a recognised possibility, but it is not permissible to make them your slaves. (147)

To consider a Guru to be a mere man, and a mere human body as Guru, is a great sin. Guru is a Tattva, not so named as a mere body. (148)

A disciple is scarce while a Guru is not. A server is rare, but not those to be served. An inquisitive person is hard to get, but not knowledge. A devotee is rare, but not God. (149)

One who seeks, money and riches, pleasure and comfort, respect and honour, worship and homage or anything from us, he could not lead us to God-realization. (150)

The world, the being and God—not to know these three is darkness. One who removes this darkness, is a Guru. (151)

The Guru is for a disciple, while the latter is not for a Guru. A ruler is for the ruled, while the subjects are not for a Rājā. (152)

God, even though a universal Guru, does never

make man his disciple, but only as a comrade and friend. (153)

A master does not grant his disciple any new knowledge, but awakens his inherent knowledge. (154)

A true Guru makes one a Guru, not a disciple, one who wants to make a disciple, he becomes a servant of the disciple. (155)

Our real Guru is within our own selves. It is discrimination, which is granted by God; who has also vouchsafed us a human body, and all spiritual means and materials. So what is the necessity of a human Guru? (156)

(XI) Anxiety

There is no need for anxiety to maintain the body, but what happens after separation from the body, it is very necessary to worry about. (157)

Whatever, has to happen will happen and whatever is not to be, would never be. Then what is to worry about? (158)

We need nothing for ourselves, for our own self lacks nothing. Whatever the body needs, is ordained according to one's fate. Then why worry about anything? (159)

God makes arrangements for our subsistence, but not for enjoyment. Therefore, have no anxiety for subsistence nor desire for enjoyment. (160)

Whatever God does, or will do, in that lies my good. Believing in this, irrespective of circumstances, one should remain free from worry. (161)

There is no unhappiness or worry due to shortage of things, but foolishness is the cause. That is removed by association with perfected souls. (162)

When a man gives up worry about his own body, by and by the world starts worrying about his body. (163)

Living with faith in God, eliminates worry of all kinds. (164)

By doing what should not be done and not doing what must be done, causes anxiety and fear. (165)

God knows better than us, is more competent and more compassionate than ourselves. So why should we worry? (166)

(XII) Warning

All materials for the dying are ready. The shroud is ready and a new one is not to be prepared. The pall bearers also are ready, and new ones have not to be born. The cremation place is ready and no new place will be required. The wood for cremation is also ready and no new trees need to be planted. One has only to wait for the last breath. As soon as the last breath is breathed, all materials would be mobilised. So, what room is there for complacency? (167)

Remember, this world is not eternal. Only the dying live here, then why are you so smug and self-satisfied about it? (168)

Ponder, would these days always remain the same forever? (169)

You make a home here, decorate it and hoard things. But, you are rushing through to death. Be prepared for the ultimate destination and make it good. (170)

For a fixed-time scheduled train also, attention is necessary from the very beginning. But the death-symbolised train has no fixed time, for that, one should remain cautious always. (171)

To do—is not certain, but to die, is. (172)

You do not see God, but God watches you without break. (173)

The incoming has to go—that is the rule. (174)

The deathly fire burns all things, then what to trust and what to wish for! (175)

Think about, who is one's own? If one were to die shortly, could anybody assist? (176)

When a birthday is celebrated we feel happy for reaching a certain age. In truth, we have not reached that age, but so many years have gone and we are short of as many years, while we are getting closer to death. (177)

When a boy is born, whether he would grow into an adult or not, whether he would get educated or not, get married or not, have a family or not, have wealth or not, in all these matters there is doubt, but in his death, there is no doubt. (178)

(XIII) Tattva-Jñāna (God-Realization)

G od-realization is transcendental. Therefore, its perception is by oneself, but not by our senses, mind and intellect etc. (179)

As long as one believes in the reality of the perishable, till then no God-realization is possible. (180)

On achieving real knowledge, faults in oneself depart and merits (special) are not perceptible. (181)

If one renounces what is not the self, then perception of our real Self dawns. (182)

An aspirant, should not have any bias—for duality or non-duality. Such bias does not lead to God-realization. (183)

So long as there is ego, there could be vanity about knowledge of God-realization, but not true realization. (184)

So long as there is attachment or aversion, one could not have God-realization. We, would only be theoretical about it.   (185)

It does not take many births to realise God; with a strong craving it may take a few minutes, as God is ever—always present.   (186)

God is not realised by practice, but by giving importance to one's discrimination. Practice brings about new conditions, but does not help realise God.   (187)

Until they realise God, all human beings are prisoners. The sign of a captive is: he sins by his own wishes and suffers from the decisions of others.   (188)

"I am Brahma." This is not realization but it is a spiritual practice known as Ahaṅgraha-Upāsanā. Therefore on God-realization there is no experience of "I am Brahma."   (189)

On realising the Truth, defects like lust and anger etc., are completely wiped out.   (190)

In our view, so long as the unreal exists, till then the faculty of discrimination functions. At the wiping out of this idea the discrimination is transformed into self knowledge.   (191)

The feeling of innocence in oneself and others, is Self-realization or liberation.   (192)

With Self-realization, man is not devoid of material environment in life but remains free from pain and pleasure.   (193)

Real knowledge does not destroy the body, but obliterates, the link with the body and annihilates ego and feeling of 'my-ness.'   (194)

Real knowledge and destruction of ignorance take place, at one time and forever.   (195)

To perceive as is, means knowledge, and to acknowledge it as it is not, is ignorance.   (196)

(XIV) Renunciation

Complete renunciation prevails only when there is absolutely no vanity about it. Pride comes when the importance of given up things is stamped on the inner faculty. Therefore, it is better to discard the importance of a thing, rather than its abandonment.   (197)

So long as, there is some interest in any person or thing truly there is no renunciation, till then.   (198)

Love, anger, myness and attachment etc., when we know how to acquire these, we also would know how to give these up. But in fact, we do not wish to do so, so we seem helpless.   (199)

Salvation is achieved by the renunciation of desire and not by giving up of things.   (200)

The body never comes to our help, but it is the giving up of 'I'-ness and 'my-ness' in the body, that helps.   (201)

The body and world, by themselves, are separating from ourselves but that does not lead to our salvation (Kalyāṇa). To give up a disjointed thing, and withdraw your 'I'ness and 'my-ness' from the same, then only you will have salvation.   (202)

By having the importance of riches in the inner faculty (mind, intellect and ego), the discarding of riches appears important. But by giving these up, one gets the vanity of renunciation, therefore, the vanity of renunciation, the importance of money signifies in our view.   (203)

By renunciation, one makes spiritual progress and things become pure. By enjoying these things, man degrades himself and such things are destroyed. (204)

Man by himself enjoys and wants others to renounce—this is not just. If he likes renunciation, then why does he not renunciate.   (205)

In reality, renunciation is that in which the vanity of renunciation is also abandoned.   (206)

(XV) Blemish

I t is open to all to have a blameless life forever, but to always have a life full of blame for anyone, is not possible. By himself, man being a fraction of God, is blameless. Faults come and go and visit him in association with, what is perishable.   (207)

An aspirant, when he observes his faults as faults, becomes sad and is unable to bear their presence. Then his faults could not continue, and God's grace destroys these faults.   (208)

Whatever blemishes exist, these arise only by giving importance to perishable things.   (209)

To cheat is a fault, but being cheated is not. (210)

By seeing divinity in everybody, all morbid feelings are destroyed.   (211)

With contentment, passion, anger and greed, all the three are destroyed.   (212)

Faults have no independent existence. The paucity of virtue is known as faults, and that lack of virtue arises by giving importance and authority to the unreal. (213)

All morbid feelings arise in the body. There is no modification in the immutable self.   (214)

The root cause of all faults is one, out of which all others arise—(i.e.) attachment with the world. Similarly, the root of all virtues, is also one, from which all good arises (i.e.) relation with God. (215)

Because of greed, essential things are not acquired, and the things acquired are not used properly. (216)

(XVI) Faulty View

Because of one's pride in his own qualities, one sees faults in others, and by noticing faults in others, one's pride gets stronger.   (217)

An aspirant wanting to remove his faults, must not look at the faults of others. He would thus reinforce his own faults, and by association, new faults would arise.   (218)

Watching the faults of others, would neither benefit ourselves, nor others.   (219)

The more impure, one's inner faculties are, the more he notices the faults of others. Like a radio, impure inner sense attracts more faults.   (220)

Should you want nobody to think of you as bad, then you have no right to think of others, as bad. (221)

By not thinking of others as bad, goodness arises from within. Goodness from within, is solid and pervasive.   (222)

If you wish to protect your innocence, do not see faults in anybody, neither in yourself nor in others. (223)

With intent to making others innocent, it is not bad to notice their faults, What is wrong, is to be happy on noting the faults of others.   (224)

The Self of all is innocent, so recognising this innocence, in children, disciples and others, and assuming the faults as transient, they should be guided, and helped to eliminate such faults.   (225)

If we assume the faults of others, they are likely to acquire these, as by noting this our own renunciation, penance and powers might contribute to the strengthening of their faults, and the persons really become faulty. We would then harm ourselves, as well. (226)

(XVII) Wealth

To think of wealth as most important, is a sign of polluted intellect. (227)

For righteousness (Dharma) one needs mind, not wealth. (228)

Wealth by itself, does not enslave man. He himself becomes a slave to wealth and thus has a fall. (229)

Because of riches nobody becomes great. On the contrary he may become a beggar. In reality great is one, who never wants anything. (230)

Whatever wealth one gets today is not due to present actions, but is a fruit of his past acts (destiny). To gain riches with the help of lies, frauds, dishonesty and thefts, as people do, would invite punishment, in the future. (231)

It is not sure, that unjustly earned wealth would be useful, but it is certain, to attract punishment. (232)

Where there is need for money, there is no godliness, on the contrary, it becomes a slavery of wealth. (233)

Just as one spends money to overcome his unhappiness, so must he spend it to remove the unhappiness of others, only then we have the right to hold such riches. (234)

For the sake of money using lies, fraud, dishonesty etc., brings about great harm and not much benefit, nor money. Whatever money comes, could then never be used fully. So, for the sake of a minor benefit, to do a great wrong, is not wise.   (235)

After one's death, man's nature goes with him, his wealth does not. He is only messing up his nature if he accumulates money, fie upon such wisdom.   (236)

On having wealth, man does not achieve independence, but he becomes dependent on money, because it is alien to him.   (237)

Even with wealth, man could be a saint, but because of desire for money, one would not become a saint.   (238)

Penury is not wiped out by getting money, but it vanishes only when the desire for money is given up.   (239)

Man's respect does not gain by increase in his wealth, but by enlarging Dharma (righteousness).
                    (240)

Material things are superior to wealth, man is superior to things, discrimination is superior to man, while God is superior to discrimination, Man's birth as a human being is for realising the Reality (God).   (241)

[(XVIII) Nāma-Japa (Chanting Divine Name)]

An aspirant might not understand anything, yet he should take refuge in God and begin with repeating God's name (Nāma-Japa).   (242)

The repetition of God's name and collective singing (chant) protects man from the hardships of Kaliyuga and helps him in his progress.   (243)

The progress in uttering of divine name is judged by incessant repetition of God's name, without any break.   (244)

The relish in Nāma-Japa lies, in actually doing it.   (245)

Nāma-Japa is not a practice, but is a cry. In routine practice, the body, senses and mind, dominate, but in a cry the primacy is of the self. (246)

Nāma-Japa nourishes all means of salvation. (247)

God's name is open to all and one has a tongue in his mouth (to take His name) and yet man goes to hell. This is very strange.   (248)

To mutter God's name after surrendering to Him, is more important, than merely taking his name. In the former case love of God has primacy, while repetition is not, as important.   (249)

Influenced by numbers, mere muttering of the name is lifeless, while it comes alive with attention fixed on God. That is why in repetition of Mantras and collective singing, the primary interest should be the love of God, as we are uttering the name of dear one. (250)

What form and name of God is greater? Rather than ask this question, an aspirant should examine himself, as to which name and form appeals and is dear to him, most. (251)

(XIX) Sin and Piety

I f anyone harms us, but really he helps us, it is because by such acts, our sins are removed. (252)

By doing wrong to others, we acquire sins, even so with hearing and speaking ill of others. (253)

By intense desire for salvation, the sins of an aspirant are eliminated. (254)

To turn one's face against God and towards the world, there is no sin so grave. (255)

"I shall not sin again", this is true penance from sin. (256)

The sins committed in human form, either in hell or going through 84 lakh births, are not exhausted and continue, and become the cause of births and deaths. (257)

Where man is happy through favourable factors, or sad due to unfavourable circumstances, there and then, he gets bound by sin and piety. (258)

To give importance to the perishable is bondage, and this leads to all sins.   (259)

If one desires happiness, even without wishing to commit a sin, yet a sin may take place. The desire for happiness induces us to sin. Therefore, if one wants freedom from sin, give up the desire for happiness.   (260)

When one wants to hurt others or has an axe to grind then sin accrues and puts one in bondage. (261)

Hiding both sin and piety—result in special fruit, so reveal your sins but not your piety. (The Rākṣasa were declining everyday and night, just like piety waned by self-statements. Rāmacaritamānasa by Tulasīdāsa—Laṅkākāṇḍa 72.2).   (262)

There is no greater virtue than turning a person towards God, and no charity like it.   (263)

To seek happiness for one's self, is the root of all sin.   (264)

"First to commit sin and then to do penance for the same knowingly", does not destroy such sin.   (265)

(XX) Path to God

E very human being has to move on the path to God, whether today or after many births; so why delay.   (266)

In seeking God, with a true heart, an aspirant secures the pleasure and kindness of all the past, present and future saints.   (267)

When an aspirant dedicates himself to God, then his mind and intellect instinctly concentrate on Him and he has not to make effort.   (268)

On the path to God, an aspirant finds, worldly favours, (money, respect, greatness, comfort etc.,) obstructive, so long as, he retains the desire or taste for elements of pleasure.   (269)

One's success or failure in worldly affairs, resulting in happiness or disappointment, does not help him to march speedily on the spiritual path. (270)

In the path to God, love and hate, are the prime enemies of an aspirant's spiritual wealth.   (271)

By any means, attach yourself to God, then He will automatically take care of you.   (272)

By moving towards God, even your worldly affairs would run smoothly, but on the worldly path, you would not realise God.   (273)

Whether you follow God, in terms of identity or diversity with God, the result would be the same. (274)

There is profit or loss in world's affairs, but in God's work there is always a profit and never a loss.   (275)

There is no companion on the worldly path, but on the spiritual path all would help you.   (276)

A selfish person even on the spiritual path, follows

his selfish interests, and a spiritual aspirant, even in worldly affairs, tries to gain success in the path of God.   (277)

With the birth of worldly desire, in God's path smoke arises. If at that stage, one is not careful then desire is strengthened. With increase in desire, the spiritual path is darkened.   (278)

The day worldly desires are wiped out, the same day longing for the divinity would be fulfilled. (279)

Dissatisfaction on a worldly subject causes a fall, but dissatisfaction on the spiritual one, leads to progress.   (280)

By 'doing' something in the world, there is advancement, but, by 'not doing' anything on the spiritual path, progress activates.   (281)

In the world of attachment, both degradation and progress remain incomplete. But in the spiritual path, there is no downfall, advancement never remains unfulfilled.   (282)

(XXI) Destiny (Prārabdha)

D estiny is for removing anxiety, but is not for making a person an idler.   (283)

Man does not commit sin or virtue by destiny, as the fruit of action is not action, but its enjoyment.   (284)

Destiny creates favourable or unfavourable conditions for pleasure or pain, but man is free to be happy or unhappy.   (285)

It is the all-knowing, the uninterested friend of all, all-powerful and all competent God's law, that nobody suffers more punishment than his sins, and that too is the fruit of some or the other of his own sins. (286)

Whatever happens, happens rightly and never wrongly. So be cautious in what you do, and be happy with what happens.   (287)

Conduct against scriptural directions does not happen by destiny, but by desire.   (288)

One thing is to 'do', and some other that 'happens', but both these are seperate matters. To 'do' is subject to effort and what 'happens' is controlled by destiny. Therefore, man is free to act in the discharge of his duties, but in securing the fruit, he is dependent on others.   (289)

(XXII) Love

L ove for God develops in a man, as soon as his attraction for the world is completely gone.   (290)

Whatever thing is yours, you like it always. So taking God as your own, love for God also develops.   (291)

How surprising, that the ever-existing changeless entity (i.e.) God is not loved, but the ever changing world appears so dear.   (292)

So long as there is attachment to the world, there is no real love for God. (293)

"The world's pleasure—giving propensity, is a special obstacle to God's love. If one renounces this propensity, then love for God would automatically arise. (294)

So long as man has an attraction for the perishable, until then, even with spiritual practice, one is not attracted by the love of non-perishable God, nor realize Him. (295)

Exclusive love for God, is called, the Rādhā Tattva. Until there is attraction for the world, the Rādhā Tattva is not intuited. (296)

There is no worship that equals the love of God. (297)

So long as an aspirant wants to carry out his own wishes, till then, he would neither love the God with attributes nor the God without attributes. (298)

God's love is not acquired by sacrifices, penance, charity, fasting pilgrimage, etc., but through regarding him firmly as his own. (299)

You do not get love from practising penance, but only achieve power. Love arises from treating God, as one's own. (300)

In the love of God, there is an exclusive rapture that is not in knowledge. Knowledge gives unbroken happiness, but love endless bliss.   (301)

Differences exist amongst sects, not in love. Love devours all differences completely.   (302)

The pull towards God is called devotion. Devotion is never complete but it keeps on increasing, more and more.   (303)

For the love of God, one must have greater closeness with Him. For His vision a fervent craving is essential.   (304)

Knowing the world, would make one a renunciate. By knowing God, greater love for Him would result.   (305)

One whose realisation is sure, love Him. Do serve the world that is sure to be separated.   (306)

That is love, where there is no impurity of personal comfort and selfishness.   (307)

Love is ahead of salvation even. Upto salvation one can relish it, but in love, one becomes the giver of bliss.   (308)

In the path of knowledge, sorrow and bondage are gone and one gets established in one self, but one achieves nothing. In the path of devotion, one acquires love which increases every moment.   (309)

Without knowledge, love passes off as delusion, and without love, knowledge is lost in nothingness. (310)

One within whom exist the previous influences of

devotion, and the shelter of divine grace, he is not satisfied by liberation alone. God's blessings dilute the taste of salvation and replace it by granting him unlimited love. (311)

No insistence on one's creed and not resorting to the disregard, rebuttal, or disrespect of another sect, after salvation, automatically helps achieve divine love. (312)

When the desire for enjoyment ends, there is fulfilment of knowledge, but there is no end to the thirst for love which is never quenched, and increases every moment. (313)

In the world, there are both attractions and repulsions (likes and dislikes), but in God there is only attraction and no repulsion at all. If there is any repulsion, then in reality, there has been no attraction. (314)

Just as from a worldly point of view, without greed for wealth, there is no special importance for the same. So without love, knowledge has no special significance and it might lead to nothingness. (315)

(XXIII) Greatness

J udging oneself great or small, in terms of created and perishable things, is a great mistake, an absurdity. (316)

To consider oneself small and others great, is greatness. To treat himself as great and others as small, is truly lowliness. (317)

A man is really great, if he makes others great. While he who makes others small, he himself is small, a slave. (318)

By wealth, lands, houses etc., material things, if one considers himself as great, it is a perversion of intellect. (319)

By taking into account worldly goods, if man treats himself as great, he is made small, by such goods. (320)

We were great earlier, then we created wealth and we treated ourselves as great, because of the wealth. This means that in fact, wealth is bigger than us. Riches get more respect and we ourselves are disgraced. (321)

(XXIV) Bondage and Salvation

Treating the body and other matters as one's own, is bondage, and not accepting them as own, means salvation. All are free to accept or reject this relationship. (322)

All relations with the world, may lead either to salvation or bondage. But the contract for the spiritual path (service to others) leads to salvation, and the link for selfishness, brings about bondage.   (323)

By maltreating a human body, man gets bound, and by its good use, he is freed. For selfish reasons, causing harm to others, is misusing the human body, while by giving up selfish interest and doing good to others, is its beneficial use.   (324)

To give importance to the perishable, is bondage.   (325)

Whatever is granted, do not accept it as your own, then salvation would come, naturally.   (326)

The world comprises the favourable and unfavourable. Man gets bound by being happy or otherwise in the favourable and unfavourable state, and in not being happy or otherwise, it liberates him.   (327)

The body is a part of the world and we ourselves are a fraction of God. So dedicate the body to the world or use it for service to the world and consecrate the self to God, then salvation occurs the same day.   (328)

By the desire for salvation, keenness for the body does not subsist. If it does, then there is no desire for salvation.   (329)

By acting for others without thought of reward, salvation comes, and acting with thought of reward for oneself, creates bondage. It means that man should act without thought of expectation in discharging his duties. (330)

If you want to free yourself from bondage, then give up the possessive spirit in acquired things, as well as, desire for not acquired ones. (331)

God's creation never binds one, nor gives pain. Man-made (I-ness and my-ness) binds and gives pain. (332)

Doing, what should not be done, and worrying about what could not be done—are two special fetters. (333)

To get a thing or not to get it, does not cause bondage, but acceptance of a link with the same, does. (334)

To treat the world for service to one's self, facilitates bondage, while beholding oneself for service to the world, is favourable for salvation. (335)

Bondage does not arise from action, but from desire. (336)

The desire for an unacquired thing and feeling of myness for the acquired, means bondage and subjugation. (337)

To renounce the desire for pleasure craving for liberation is necessary. But to seek liberation with desire for the same, becomes an impediment. (338)

Man does not get bound by his actions as such,

but by the attachment and selfishness inherent in his
actions.   (339)

By associating selfishness with any action, such an
act becomes lowly and causes bondage.   (340)

It is a principle that, until man keeps on acting for
himself, he does not exhaust the acts and gets bound
by them.   (341)

So long as there is a link with nature, till then
to act or not to act, both are acts which create
bondage.   (342)

Salvation is of the soul and not of the body. On
achieving salvation, the body does not separate from
the world, only the self, remains separate from the
body and the world.   (343)

Salvation does not come from outside
renunciation, but by inward detachment.   (344)

"I do not have to take anything"—only with this,
I could gain salvation.   (345)

Liberation is easy and natural, bondage is subject
to doings.   (346)

In reality, it is the liberated that achieves
salvation—a bounded one does not.   (347)

[(XXV) Giving up Evils]

A n aspirant should not consider anybody as
wicked, nor talk ill of anybody, nor think ill
of anybody, nor see ill in anybody, nor hear of

anybody's ill, or speak ill to anybody. By following these six dont's firmly, an aspirant becomes free from wickedness. (348)

Should anybody do wrong, but in return do not wish ill of him, think as if one cuts his own tongue by his teeth. (349)

It is not necessary to do as much good, as there is need to give up one's own wickedness. By giving up wickedness, good would come about by itself, and would not have to be resorted to. (350)

Whatsoever, we think good, it is not obligatory for us to fully carry it out but what we consider as an evil, we are bound to completely shun it. To avoid it strength, ability, knowledge and courage, are granted to us by God. (351)

Courage does not lie in doing good, but in not doing ill of anybody. (352)

One who wants salvation for oneself, he should have no ill-will towards anybody. (353)

By having ill-will against anybody, whether harm is caused to him or not, is not sure, but our own inner faculty would be sullied. (354)

Remember: Should you harm anybody, then he must be expected to be harmed, but you would be guilty of a new sin. (355)

By doing good, limited good occurs, but by giving up ill-will, unlimited good results. (356)

To be good, we do not have to do anything special, only we must give up ill-will altogether, and we shall become good. (357)

(XXVI) Devotee

Through a devotee of God acts do not take place, but there is worship every moment, as in each of his acts he has a feeling of worship. (358)

One whose mind is concentrated on God, he should not be considered to be an ordinary individual, as he is a member of Almighty's court. (359)

Just as a greedy person's eyes are fixed on money, so must a devotee's eyes be always set on God. (360)

The Devas bestow on their worshippers their desired things, (after their worship is accomplished) without thought of good or bad, but God Almighty, grants to the devotees, by His own wish things, which are of great benefit to them. (361)

You become the servant of God, then He would make you a master. (362)

God's devotee may come from howsoever low a caste, yet he is greater than a devotionless learned Brāhmaṇa. (363)

In God's heart, there is so much respect for His devotee, and there is none else, He respects more. (364)

A devotee who sees nothing special in himself, nor is proud of anything in himself, God's exceptionality is dominant in such a devotee. (365)

A devotee surrendered to God, has not to offer worship, because through him and by himself, automatically worship is conducted. (366)

In whatever form a devotee wishes to view God, He, by the devotee's feelings appears accordingly to him. (367)

To call God's devotee as a "Devatā", is to denigrate him, as his status is much higher than the 'Devas'. (368)

Devotees, who love God, are not attracted by God's majesty, but are impelled by His ownness toward them. (369)

Lovers' feelings are understood by lovers, a knower does not, and an unknowing one, never at all. (370)

A devotee attains bliss while serving God, and God also feels bliss in the service of devotees. (371)

(XXVII) God

G od or the universal soul, is reality, and the rest is all unreal. (372)

Until there is influence of the world on the inner faculties, till then it is difficult to understand the importance of God. (373)

God is knowable, not by mind, intellect and senses, but by the self. (374)

Whatever thing is treated as the farthest from us, the body is still farther and whatever we think of as the nearest, God is nearer than that also. (375)

Everything receivable by us, leaves us, but ever attained God is never lost whether we feel it so or not. (376)

The world is a non-reality. God who is devoid of all actions is ever existent. It is by whose reality that the unreal world looks real. (377)

We attribute 'Isness' (Reality) to the world not to the God, this is a mistake. (378)

Nobody makes his servant his master in the world, but God makes His surrendered devotee as master, such magnanimity rests only with God. (379)

Except God, there is nothing else which could always remain with us and we ever with Him. (380)

Faith in the ever changing world, does not allow us to have belief in God. (381)

Just as the Sun rises and is not born, so also God manifests Himself on incarnation but is not born like us. (382)

God exists, such acknowledgement is sufficient. What is God like, it is not necessary to know. (383)

God, even though omnipotent, yet is unable to be

away from us.   (384)

Where is God? He is there, where, here or there
are no more applicable. It means God is beyond space,
time thing, person etc.   (385)

God is present everywhere, but there ought to be
an ardent seeker. There are so many pillars but they
need Prahlāda.   (386)

There is no deficiency of God anywhere, but there
is a shortage of people who long to see Him. (387)

One who sets his sights on the world, He asks
'where is God?' And one who has set his eyes on God,
he says, 'Where does God not exist?'   (388)

Just as the Sun is not covered by the clouds, but
our eyes are covered by clouds. So is God not
concealed, but our intellect is.   (389)

God does not wish to make man His slave, but
He desires to make him a companion (equal to
Himself).   (390)

Sat (the real) is not opposed to Asat (the unreal)
rather gives it a status. It is the quest of the Sat that
devours Asat.   (391)

We cannot behold untruth without truth and
without untruth we could not describe truth.   (392)

God cannot be described, but it is realized. (393)

Except God, whatever else is acceptable, there is
as much ignorance about it.   (394)

To treat oneself as an orphan, in spite of the presence of Lord of the world, is a mistake.   (395)

Man should have faith only in God. If he has faith in the world and discernment in God, then he would turn into an atheist.   (396)

In the beginning, to an aspirant God appears to be far off, then He seems closer, then he notices Him within himself and later he sees nothing, but God.   (397)

There are beings within God, and the world within the being. But God has an independent status, while the world and the beings have no independent existence of their own.   (398)

Beyond the entire country, time, activity, things, people, conditions, circumstances, occurrences etc., even in their non-existence, whatever remains as residue, that is God.   (399)

(XXVIII) God's Grace

J ust as cow's milk is not for the cow itself, but for others, so is the grace of God not for God, but is for all others (us).   (400)

If you want God's blessings, so be kind to smaller persons than yourself, then God would be kind. If you desire kindness, without being kind to others, this is unjust and disparaging to your knowledge.   (401)

The Gītā, that Arjuna could not get to hear the

second time, that Gītā, we read and listen to everyday. That is God's exceptional kindness.   (402)

Upto date, all the saints that we have had, were by God's grace, liberated, knowers of the essence and lovers of God, and not so by their own efforts. (403)

Achieving of the self evident Supreme Abode of God, does not come even by own actions, efforts and discipline but only by the grace of God.   (404)

(XXIX) Attaining God

M an desirous of attaining God, with a true heart, may belong to any caste, creed, stage of life, sect or condition, or be a great sinner or of bad character, he is entitled fully to attain God.   (405)

An aspirant should have no expectations from the world, which is not everlasting and he should be never without hope in God, because He is never non-existent.   (406)

To be contented with regard to God, and to be dissatisfied with the world, is most harmful.   (407)

Just as a fish without water is upset, similarly, if we were to get uneasy without God, then there would be no delay in attaining God.   (408)

On attaining God, there is nothing more to do or to know, and nothing more to get. In that lies the success of human life and its fulfilment.   (409)

An aspirant must realise, that God exists

everywhere. Therefore He is also here; God exists at all times, therefore is present now. He exists in all and as such, exists in the self; belongs to all and He therefore is mine also. (410)

In attaining God, restlessness brings quicker results than any other thought out spiritual practice. (411)

Not having a keen longing in one's self, causes delay in the attainment of God. (412)

In a game, if a boy is spotted by another he has to present himself and not to remain hidden any more. So as God is hidden everywhere, if an aspirant perceives him everywhere, then God would not be hidden, but would reveal Himself. (413)

By turning away from all other sides, an aspirant attains his beloved God, within himself. (414)

Attainment of God is easy, not through action, but by longing. (415)

For attaining Him if God has bestowed a human form on man, He has also granted Him full competence and other means alongwith, so much so, that man could in his life attain God many times. (416)

Because of deficiency in earnest longing, delay occurs in God's attainment, but not because of inadequacy of effort. (417)

God's relations are marked by equality with each caste, stage of life, sect, order, so wherever one is situated, he can attain God.   (418)

Having taken refuge in unreality and through unreality
to desire achieve reality, is a great mistake.   (419)

For the purpose one receives the human body, if
it is difficult to achieve that objective, but what is
easy?   (420)

What should be done to see God ? One could chant
His name and beg of God that "I do not forget Him."
By that our love for God would increase and then God
would appear.   (421)

So long as there remains the wish to 'do' or to
'gain' anything, till then, one does not perceive the
eternal God.   (422)

God's attainment results only after fervent desire.
For not having such a desire, the main reason is, the
wish for enjoyment of worldly pleasure.   (423)

In the Satyayuga etc., whatever Godly attainment
was achieved by the great saints, the same is available
today to all, in the Kaliyuga also.   (424)

The satisfaction of pleasure is not forever, nor for
all, but the attainment of God is open to all, and
for all times.   (425)

In the attainment of God, there is primacy of
feelings and not of action.   (426)

God is not attained by obstinacy, but by true
devotion.   (427)

In the attainment of God, man importantly needs spiritual feelings and good conduct, but not high caste or creed. (428)

There is primacy of discrimination, feelings and renunciation (of attachment) in attaining God, but not so much of action. (429)

Where there is a beginning and an end for each act, so how could its fruit be without end. So God is not action-oriented. (430)

Keen desire for attaining God, creates the burning fire of separation, which destroys the sins of unlimited births and enables attainment of God. (431)

The absence of keen desire for God-attainment, primarily results from worldly pleasures, hopes and enjoyment. (432)

Ordinarily, if anything could be equally secured by all, that is God. Excepting God, nothing could normally be acquired by everyone. (433)

We cannot achieve anything except God and, whatever else is acquired, would go away in nothingness. (434)

God can only be realized when the following five are not favourable—"enjoyment of sense-objects, sleep, laughter, love of the world, and much talk." (435)

An aspirant takes longer to achieve God, for the

reason that he tolerates the separation from God. If this segragation were to have no support, then there is no delay in the achievement of God.   (436)

So long as there is desire for untruth, its refuge and trust, till then truth is not perceived.   (437)

Attachment for God is truly not difficult, but due to lack of ardent desire it becomes so.   (438)

God does not insist on action, but demands feelings—'**Bhāvagrāhī Janārdanaḥ**'. By Godly feelings (single minded devotion) God grants His view (Darśana) but not by action.   (439)

By cutting of links with ephemeral things, the permanent essence, is automatically intuited by the self.   (440)

Man has a right to attain God and under every circumstance he can achieve Godhood.   (441)

It does not take long to attain God—only time in giving up the desire for sensual pleasures.   (442)

If there be exclusive longing for God, then God would reveal Himself or if, there are no other desires, He would still reveal Himself, but there should be no incompleteness in this.   (443)

Know the 'Sat' or you might not; what you know as Asat, shun it, then you would attain the Sat. (444)

To achieving God, man is as much free, as in no other work.   (445)

Not many means are required for attaining God, but inner devotion is essential.   (446)

God does not meet a Brāhmaṇa, Kṣatriya, Vaiśya, Śūdra, celibate, householder, recluse or a Saṁnyāsī, but he meets a devotee.   (447)

In acquiring wealth, action is dominant, but for achieving God, longing is important.   (448)

The attainment of God, is not a fruit of action, but is one of grace, however the desire rests with oneself.   (449)

The world is incomplete and we acquire it as incomplete. God is complete and meets as complete.   (450)

One who has not attained God, he has done nothing, done nothing and done nothing.   (451)

In attaining God, the greatest hindrance is of desire for enjoyment and accumulation of things. By sharing the joy of others, the desire for pleasure is wiped out and by sharing the unhappiness of others, the craving for accumulation is lost.   (452)

The world is ever-changing and to trust such a world and accept it as real, is the main impediment to God-realisation.   (453)

The attraction for pleasure born of contact is the prime obstacle to the perception of an ever-attained God.   (454)

In seeking God, things do not overshadow, but the importance of things has created a screen. (455)

Acting in selfish interest and accepting one's close link with the inert (like body etc.,) the achievement of God— though all pervading, is obstructed. (456)

God is all pervasive in space and times etc. In accepting the world as real, man realises the distance between himself and God. (457)

No circumstances are factors for the attainment of God, and no circumstances are obstructive in realising Him, as God is beyond all circumstances. (458)

God is not far off, only the pull of desire is weak. (459)

The world exists, exists now and is ours—so by accepting that—God is, exists now and is ours—this perception is not possible. (460)

An aspirant admits that "God exists," but that the "world does not exist", this he does not acknowledge. It is because of this, obstacles arise in attaining God. (461)

By accepting the insistence of one path and opposing other paths, there arise great obstructions in fulfilment of our goal. (462)

If we attach importance in our heart to anything except God, then the same, impedes in God-realisation. (463)

Faith in God, is even greater than God, though God exists always at all places, we do not see Him, but by faith we meet Him. (464)

God is consciousness, only our gaze is not there. (465)

"If we do something then we will achieve God," this attitude would strengthen our bodily ego. What we gain by action, would be impermanent. (466)

In renouncing the world, 'discrimination' helps; what assists in God's realisation, is faith. (467)

In reality, God is ever-existent, the Guru also is, so is the knowledge of the Self, in addition are competence and capability in oneself. It is because of attachment to ephemeral pleasure, there is obstruction to the revelation of God. (468)

The body can deal with worldly affairs, and render service, but it cannot attain God. After detachment from the body, God-realisation can be achieved through the self and to the self. (469)

(XXX) Turning Away from God

O n turning away from God, man perceives his unfulfilment in doing, knowing and acquiring. (470)

Without turning away from God, no worldly pleasure could be enjoyed, and man necessarily turns his face away from God by cherishing and enjoying worldly pleasure. (471)

By turning his face away from God, man becomes an orphan. (472)

Those who do not know the world, get caught in the world, and those who do not know God, they turn away from God. (473)

On desiring to get something from this world, we soon turn away from God. (474)

(XXXI) Relation with God (Ownness)

As much man accepts his relationship with worldly things, persons etc., so much more he becomes subservient to others. If man were to acknowledge his link only with God, he would be free for all times. (475)

If an aspirant considering himself of God, renders service to the world; he will be serving both the world and God properly. But considering himself belonging to the world, he serves the world in that case he will not be properly serving even the world, what to talk of God. (476)

God is our own, but not for ourselves, as we are for God. The meaning is, that we do not desire anything from God, but we offer ourselves to Him. Taking the worst circumstances, we ought to treat these happily as God's offerings.   (477)

For good use only things are ours, and God is one's own to give to oneself. So use things for the world and offer yourself to God.   (478)

A husband can die, he could give up his wife; even then on going to a new home, a daughter has no worry. But God neither dies, nor ever gives one up. Therefore on establishing a link with God, why worry? God knows how to hold, but not to give up.   (479)

"I belong to God and God is mine"—there is no competence, no worthiness and no rightfulness etc., that equals God's ownness.   (480)

A devotee should not look at his own capacity etc., but constantly watch at his ownness of God. (481)

Ownness with God is the easiest and the best means to reach God.   (482)

There is nobody mine, except God, this is true devotion.   (483)

Though all powerful, God is unable to distance itself from us.   (484)

God is mine, and everything given is not mine, but is God's.   (485)

Man treats material things and actions as his own, and always becomes subservient to them. When he treats God as his own and completely surrenders to Him, then he always becomes free.   (486)

Our relation with God is intrinsic and natural. For this we do not need any power, ability, or assistance etc., from others.   (487)

Just as we have accepted the relation with the world, that it is available, and near. Similarly, we acknowledge the link with God. And as we believe the link with God is not available and is far off, the same way we should treat the relation with the world.   (488)

Just believe that "I am of God." If you accept that 'I am of the world', then you will forget God not only while doing work of the world even when you are engaged in His worship.   (489)

Howsoever you may be, believe now, this moment that, "I am of God."   (490)

Instead of meditating on God, it is better to develop one's ownness with God. One's ownness will lead automatically to meditation. Automatic meditation is the best.   (491)

God loves one's ownness more, not so much renunciation or penance etc.   (492)

The way to turn towards God, is by complete turning away from the world.   (493)

A firm one's ownness with God, swallows all faults.   (494)

Until there is linkage with God, everything remains worldly. Once one's ownness is established, everything becomes divine. (495)

Should we seek anything from God, then our link is with that thing, and not with God. (496)

One who is our own, he is ever-existent in ourselves. Only it is to be confirmed. Who is not our own, keeps on separating from us always, and it is only necessary to deny it. (497)

Man's relations with God is obvious and direct. In this, there is no need for an agent or intermediary. (498)

(XXXII) Mind

It is not too necessary to fix your mind on God, as it is to devote oneself to God. If one is well attracted to God, then the mind would by itself be fixed in Him. (499)

As much concentration of mind is necessary in the path of Yoga, it is not so in the path of devotion. In devotion, there must be firmness of our relationship with God. (500)

Peace comes from renunciation, not from concentration of mind. (501)

Making the mind steady is not valuable, but the awareness of the independent and steady existence of the Self is valuable. (502)

The need to remove the attraction of the world from the mind is greater, than wiping out the fickleness of mind. (503)

So long as there is a tendency of removing the mind from the world and directing the same to God, till then there would be no controlling of mind. Mind could be controlled only when there is no acceptance of the existence of anything else, except God. (504)

By unselfish feelings, the intellect becomes steady and by practice the mind. Liberation comes by the steadiness of intellect, but not from the steadiness of mind. The steadiness of mind endows one with occult powers. (505)

The identity of mind is not with God but with nature. Therefore, mind can be merged in God, but cannot be fixed on Him. (506)

(XXXIII) Man

To enjoy happiness there is heaven and for suffering there is hell. To rise above happiness and suffering, and for doing the highest good to oneself, the means is the human body. (507)

In reality, human birth is the beginning and the end of all births. If man achieves salvation then it is his last birth and if he does not, then it is the beginning of his endless births. (508)

Uplifting of the Self or attaining God is man's own duty, as a human body has been granted to man, entirely for his salvation. (509)

Accepting the relationship with human body, and enjoying pleasure and accumulation of things, is not man's duty, but is alien to him. (510)

By human form alone, one does not become a human being. Man is one who gives due importance to his discrimination (Viveka). (511)

If man is not human, then he is inferior to animals, for the reason that, animals by reaping the fruits of past sinful actions, are preparing to become human beings, and man by new acts of sins, prepares for hell and to be an animal. (512)

The highest state of salvation, is natural to man. (513)

The proper use of a body, is only in the service of the world. (514)

To remember God and to serve others, these two establish humanity, in man. (515)

If one is granted a human body, and it does not achieve God, it is a matter for sorrow and pain. (516)

Man's body is not for hearing and learning only, but for realizing the blessedness. Hearing and learning comes to animals and birds also, like those who work in a circus. (517)

One who does not serve others, nor remember God, he is not entitled to be called a human being. (518)

To watch for the start of pleasure is beastly, and to realise its result is humanity. (519)

The creation has been formed in such a way, that the life of a man is for others, not for his self. (520)

Without attaining God, human body is worthless. (521)

One who is attracted to God, he is fortunate and great. He is entitled to be called a human being. (522)

For the success of human life, it is essential, all the time, to be extremely careful. (523)

The importance of human body depends on discrimination and not on action. (524)

In reality, man's body is not action-oriented, but it is a means. One who is not an aspirant, could either be a Deva or a demon, but not a human being. (525)

'Man' is one, who has a birthright to attaining God. (526)

(XXXIV) The Feeling of Mine

So long as man's feelings of mine for his wife and son persist, it would be impossible for him to reform them, because such feelings are the impurity at the root. (527)

When man with a possessive spirit retains so many worldly materials, he maintains a link with Asat (unreality). This grade of relationship causes him to have that grade of downfall.   (528)

Whatever things we treat as our own, we become dependent on them. A dependant person could not attain happiness, even in a dream—'**Parādhīna Sapanehu Sukhu Nāhīm**'.   (529)

The world is of God, but in error man treats it as his own, that is why he gets tied down.   (530)

A body, its senses etc., never say, that we are yours and you are ours; only we treat these as ours and this acceptance is an impurity (**Mamatā Mala Jari Jāi**).   (531)

We do not get caught by living in a house, but get trapped by accepting the house, as ours.   (532)

As man, accepts many things as his own and for himself, so much he gets ensnared by them.   (533)

When a man treats as many things in the world as his own, he becomes subservient to them. But in accepting God as his own, he becomes free.   (534)

It is a great mistake to treat the body etc., as one's own and for 'oneself'. If the mistake is eliminated, then there is no doubt, in one's receiving benediction.   (535)

If we cannot live forever with somebody, nor could it stay with us always. To treat that body as our own, one would be disappointed and shed tears, for it. So one should not treat that body as own, but offer service to the same.   (536)

One who treats a thing received, as his own, is neither good for the world, the self, nor God. (537)

A man without the sense of mine can do much good for the world, as compared with one who has such feelings. (538)

Neither accept anything as one's own, nor for oneself. Do not desire for anything; as treating a thing as one's own, imparts impurity to it and its desire means loss of peace. (539)

The world is moving away every moment. The feeling of mine for the departing leads to sorrow, but such feeling for the eternal God, would result in your beatitude, forever. (540)

My, so-called things, can never remain ever with me, then what is the difficulty in giving up their 'Myness'? (541)

To accept the body as ours, only gives us unhappiness and to treat it as belonging to the world, grants salvation. (542)

A thing that separates from us, does not belong to us. What separates is a thing that, in reality, is separate from us. (543)

To accept our body as our own, is to accept the company of 'Asat' (untruth), and not to accept it as own, is association of 'Sat'. (544)

If we accept the body as our own, then we shall notice things happening in body as happening in ourselves and see things touching the body as reaching the self. (545)

(XXXV) Death and Immortality

The body-world linkage creates a perception of death, and a connection with God, that of immortality. (546)

An act for oneself, first it links with the act and then with its fruit. The act and fruit both, after these arise are destroyed, but whatever attachment remains in the inner faculty, creates a cycle of births and deaths. (547)

To treat the body as 'I' or 'mine' is an error. Such error itself is death. (548)

It is not certain, that a thing may or may not happen, but death is wholly inevitable. (549)

Just as death is easy for the body, so is immortality easy, for the self. (550)

(XXXVI) Union and Pleasure (Yoga & Bhoga)

Being happy under pleasant conditions and unhappy under painful ones, makes a person a pleasure seeker and not a 'Yogī', (trying for spiritual

union). A 'Yogī' remains equanimous in both pain
and pleasure.   (551)

A pleasure seeker is sick, unhappy and is
doomed.   (552)

No person, happy with his own pleasure, can be a
'Yogī'.   (553)

A seeker of pleasure, is not a spiritual aspirant
(Yogī), but is a sick person, (**Bhoge roga-bhayam**). (554)

Union of two things etc., leads to enjoyment and
'Yoga' (permanent linkage with God) happens singly
and automatically. So long as pleasure is sought, till
then 'Yoga' could not be perceived. Only on the full
renunciation of pleasure, 'Yoga' (union) could be felt
and on achieving 'Yoga' the desire for pleasure is
wiped out, completely.   (555)

The association of God leads to 'Yoga' and linkage
with the world results in enjoying pleasure.   (556)

To derive pleasure from solitude and to enjoy the
concentration of mind is enjoyment (Bhoga), but not
spiritual union (Yoga).   (557)

To establish links with the world is Bhoga, but
breaking those links is called 'Yoga'.   (558)

Being agreeable under any condition is Bhoga. By
Bhoga, one's individuality is not lost. An aspirant
should not be willing to accept any complacence with
the condition.   (559)

Separation from the world also is automatic, so is the union with God. (560)

To give up the desire for the contact of that which separates apart by itself is called 'Yoga' or union. (561)

One, who is sometimes a 'Yogī' and at other times a pleasure seeker, he is in reality a 'Bhogī' (enjoyer). (562)

A "Yogī' brings happiness to all, but a 'Bhogī' causes unhappiness to all. (563)

'That I should get something is 'Bhoga', and that others might receive it, is "Yoga". (564)

One who seeks his own happiness and comfort, is a "Bhogī", and not a "Yogī". (565)

What is forever and for everybody and its achievement, is 'Yoga' and what is not eternal, nor for everyone, its acquisition is 'Bhoga'. (566)

To accept God as one's own is 'Yoga', and desiring something of God is 'Bhoga'. (567)

'Yoga' is the result of separation (from the world) and 'Bhoga' comes from contact with sense objects. (568)

A pleasure seeker (Bhogī) is obligated to many, while a Yogī is indebted to none. (569)

(XXXVII) Attachment and Hatred

A ttachment and hatred are transient morbid feelings of our inner faculties, but not natural tendencies (Dharma). Dharma is natural and permanent, while the changes are temporary (i.e.,) these come and go. As attachment and hatred are intermittent conditions of our inner faculties (mind, intellect and ego), these can be wiped out.   (570)

An aspirant's activity and absence from activity should not be in terms of attraction and hatred, but must be in accord with the scriptures (Śāstras).   (571)

Actions taken under the influence of attraction and hatred, do not result in good.   (572)

The tendency of hatred towards other aspirants is a great impediment in the path of one's success. (573)

Discrimination is eternal (beginningless), but attraction is self-created. Attraction of the world overwhelms discrimination and with the development of discrimination attachment goes away.   (574)

By accepting the ever-changing world as permanent, the duality of attraction and hatred etc., are born.   (575)

Whatever we like, we notice no faults in it and whatever we dislike, we see nothing good in it. Only on renunciation of like and dislike, do we see the same thing, in its true form.   (576)

In truth, everything is divine, but because of like and dislike, it appears as inert. If like and dislike were absent, then there exists nothing except divinity (God).   (577)

(XXXVIII) Give and Take

B y seeking happiness, the inner faculty becomes impure and by giving happiness, it acquires piety.   (578)

Whosoever seeks something from the worldly ocean, he gets drowned in it, and one who parts with his things, he crosses it.   (579)

By wishing to give something, brings unity and amity to society, and the desire to take something from it, results in conflict.   (580)

The attitude of 'giving' leads to spiritual progress, while feelings of 'taking' brings about a fall.   (581)

Treating a body as 'I', 'mine' and 'for me', feelings of 'taking' things, arise.   (582)

Maintain relations with others, only to serve them. Should you retain relations to seek something, then you will face unhappiness.   (583)

To give away in charity after taking it, is not as good, as not taking at all.   (584)

Not taking anything, is a greater act of virtue comparatively, than receiving it and then giving it away. However, there are few people, who can understand this.   (585)

It is a sin to take anything from this world, but to give it away, is pious.   (586)

To make ourselves happy, even our body is not ours and to give happiness to others (by service), the entire world is ours.   (587)

The desire for 'taking' makes man a slave and only by the wish to 'give', one becomes a master.   (588)

The feelings for taking something makes it a 'Bhoga', and the wish to give it away is 'Yoga'. (589)

The body has to be provided with water, food, clothing, as necessary, but one should not be a recepient of these things by establishing a bond with the body. 'Taking' is bondage, while 'giving' is salvation.   (590)

(XXXIX) Surrender (Refuge)

B y taking refuge with the world, one becomes subservient, and in taking shelter under God, one acquires freedom.   (591)

Without taking refuge in God, it is impossible to know Him.   (592)

By surrendering only to God and not taking shelter in anybody else, is exclusive devotion. (593)

Dependence on the world, is an obstruction for surrender to God. (594)

Fear arises from others, not from our own. God is our own. By surrendering to God, man becomes fearless for all times. (595)

On accepting the shelter of God, a devotee should have no doubts, no checks, no contrary feelings, nor touch- stone tests. (596)

The recognition of constant relationship with God, means the surrender to God. On his surrender, the devotee becomes free from worry, fear, sorrow and doubt. (597)

Giving up all selfish desires for God, is surrender to Him. (598)

Surrender is not of the mind and intellect, but of the self. (599)

There is no greater refuge than that of God. (600)

Surrender and fortune "both these result in giving up of worries, not of efforts (i.e., scripturally ordained action). (601)

Living beings are manifestly a fraction of God. As long as they do not take the refuge of God, of whom they are a fraction and surrender to others, they would become subservient and suffer. (602)

Until man takes the refuge of God, till then no assistance whatever would sustain him and he would continue to suffer. (603)

One who is not vain about his spiritual practice and who sees no other means of his blessedness (Kalyāṇa), he is surely entitled to seek the refuge of God. (604)

We should take the haven of one, who is not separate, distant, facing away from us and could not be parted with. (605)

If one sees anything special in himself, that could obstruct him in surrendering to God. (606)

The essence of the Vedas is in the Upaniṣads, the Gītā is the essence of the Upaniṣads and the essence of the Gītā is to surrender to God. (607)

So long as one is vain of his own power, till then there could be no surrender to God. (608)

Surrender is easy, but for a vain person, it is difficult. "I can do anything", this vanity, so long as it persists, will make surrender hard. (609)

By surrendering to God, one achieves God, which could not be attained by mere effort. (610)

From all points of view, there is no better way, than complete surrender to God alone. (611)

(XL) Saints and Great Souls

To make your life according to the advice given by saints and great souls, is rendering true service to them.   (612)

Just as the sun gives light to all equally, so through the saints and great souls, all benefit uniformly.   (613)

Outward light is granted by the sun, while the inner light comes from saints and great souls. (614)

The greatest service to the saints and high souls, is to mould your life to accord with their principles—the reason being, that they value their principles more than their lives.   (615)

God, saints and great souls, righteousness (Dharma) and Śāstras these do not ever turn away from anybody. It is only man who is disinclined towards them.   (616)

Nobody could take out mustard from the sea, but the saints have extracted the Gītā, from the world's scriptures and given it to us, which is a most unusual kindness.   (617)

There are five means by which to get benefit from God—repetitive naming (Nāma-Japa), meditation, service, obedience and company, but from saints only three (i.e.) service, obedience and company are available.   (618)

A wealthy man makes others like servants, but the saints make others also into saints. (619)

God, saints, virtuous and persons of good thought, never disappoint an aspirant, but help him to progress. (620)

The greatest reform of society is brought about by a detached saint. (621)

Saints—great souls do not come to the world to attract people to themselves, but to draw them towards God. Those who live for enticing people to themselves (for their worship and meditation), they are anti-God and would go to hell. (622)

(XLI) The World

Whatever union (Saṁyoga) that exists in the world, is continuously being destroyed by the fire of separation. Whatever creates union, assuredly results in separation. The mistake lies in the fact, that the union is taken as permanent. (623)

The link with the world must certainly lead to separation, but reunion with the separated element is not sure. Hence the separation of the world is a fact. (624)

By the linkage with perishable materials, one's sorrow could never be removed. (625)

The created and perishable things should not gain mastery over oneself (i.e.) not taking recourse to these, means man's real victory. (626)

So long as dependence on the body and world, does not totally vanish, till then the hope to live, the fear of death, the attachment for action and greed for receiving; these four, are not eliminated. (627)

Man himself establishes a link with the world through attachment but the world by itself does not ever do so. (628)

By mixing with the world, the knowledge of the world is not attained. By remaining aloof from God, the knowledge of God is not achieved—this is a principle. (629)

Union with the world and separation from God are only accepted by mistake. (630)

By acknowledging one's link with the perishable, the inner faculty, action and materials, all three become impure, and by breach of the relationship, all three become pure, automatically. (631)

So long there is a link with the world, till then there is enjoyment of pleasure (Bhoga), but not union (Yoga). By giving up worldly union from one's mind, always 'Yoga' is accomplished successfully, meaning that one feels the realisation of natural union with God. (632)

By giving up the accepted relationship with the world, either the granted (body etc.) materials are treated as of the world and used in the service of the world or giving up links with the inert (body etc.) material, one could establish oneself in the Self or surrender oneself alongwith the body to God.   (633)

By taking retreat in the created perishable things and in linking with these and seeking happiness, man can never gain happiness—this is a rule.   (634)

The slavery of the perishable does not permit one to turn toward the immortal (God).   (635)

The materials of the world are for the world, and not for our use.   (636)

The world is not worthy of trust, but worthy for rendering service.   (637)

Sense of mine with the perishable, one gets inquietude and bondage.   (638)

Even   after knowing untruth as not truth, the attraction of untruth is not wiped out, and till then truth is not realised. (Just as while noting the unreality of a movie picture, its attraction is still retained.) (639)

Just as God's auspices leads to the highest good, so dependence on the perishables of the world, like wealth etc., brings about a fall.   (640)

To give importance to any material thing, is the root of misfortune.   (641)

One should only have faith in God, one is deceived in putting faith in created and perishable things and then suffer pain.   (642)

We cannot be separated from God and could not ever be united with the world.   (643)

We cannot forever live with the world, nor separate from God ever.   (644)

By being associated with untruth, all faults and antipathies arise.   (645)

Continuous change in the body and the world, teaches us a practical lesson, that your link is with the unchangeable essence (God). It is not with the changeable, we cannot exist with you, nor you with us.   (646)

Presently, those things, and persons that are with us, how long would they keep our company? Everybody would have necessarily to think of this.   (647)

We wish to keep our body, our happiness and comfort and fulfil our hearts' desire—this is all a dependance on 'Asat'.   (648)

What exists sometime and not at another, exists somewhere or not, exists in something or not, belongs to somebody or not, in reality does not exist. (649)

Things and persons do not continue, but the accepted relationship with these is retained. This acknowledged relationship is the cause of births and deaths.   (650)

The world is moving away in its own mode. We

ourselves try to catch it (while it is going) and then we cry over its separation. (651)

One who does not concern himself with the world, the world takes notice of him. But one who cares for the world, the world throws him away, after sucking him dry. (652)

So long as man maintains a link with worldly matter and considers these, as necessary, till then he will never be happy. (653)

By conceding the distinct existence of the world, union and separation result and by giving importance to this, pain and pleasure come about. (654)

The entity of the world, is not an impediment, but the effect of the importance given to it is, the impact of which might lead to slavery. (655)

Union with the world is temporary and separation is permanent. It is the duty of man to accept what is permanent. (656)

Whatever worldly things, we attach much importance to only succeed in impeding to our realisation of God and these things by themselves also do not stay on. (657)

The world may be real or unreal, but our link with it is unreal—this is without any doubt. (658)

The world is like a leaf of henna, green from outside, but full of the red colour of God, inside. (659)

We in ourself are living and imperishable, and worldly objects are inert and destructibles. Both classes are different. So how could we get a thing from a different class?   (660)

Just as the sun after rising, moves continuously to set, so after creation, the world continues to pass on to nothingness.   (661)

The world is of different class and there could be no link with such class, only a mere acceptance of a link with it. This acknowledgement leads to unfortunate result. When this is wiped out, salvation comes automatically.   (662)

The charm of worldly materials, self esteem, greatness, appreciation, comfort, respect etc., is a cause for a fall.   (663)

What does not exist, to accept it as an entity and to desire its acquisition or destruction, is to keep company with 'Asat' (untruth).   (664)

Attachment for a thing, person or act, makes a person subservient. Detachment with these, could make him free.   (665)

So long as the inert world would exercise influence on a person, one must assume his stay in the inert, but not in God.   (666)

A body by forgetting the world (as in sleep) gets rest, and if there is complete separation from these (body and world) then one achieves the great repose.   (667)

It is necessary to ponder over for detaching oneself from the body and the world, but not to undertake any practice.   (668)

In the limitless universe, there is nothing our own, nor meant for us.   (669)

Whatever is non-existent at any space, time, act, thing, person, condition, circumstance happening, etc., is never existent at all, in other words it is always non-existent and it is 'Asat'—नासतो विद्यते भाव: (Gītā II. 16).   (670)

(XLII) Good and Bad Qualities

A ll the evil propensities and immoral practices are made so by man, but not by God. God is truth and these are untrue. How could untruth be created by truth?   (671)

By turning away from the world, even without making effort, good qualities follow.   (672)

When a person turns toward God, then he achieves all good qualities. And when he is face to face with the world, then he acquires bad qualities.   (673)

If saddened by his own helplessness and having faith in the grace of God, whatever bad qualities man wants to remove, would be given up and whatever good qualities he wishes to acquire, he would surely gain. (674)

Good qualities and good conduct lead to vanity, if these are accepted as within one's self. But bad qualities and conduct get strengthened, if treated as belonging to the self. (675)

(XLIII) Good and Bad Company

B y keeping the company of pious people, man gains more than even meditation in solitude. (676)

In virtuous company, even without effort one rises higher, and by bad company, even without doing anything, he falls. (677)

Without giving up the association of unholy, there is no obvious gain from good company. (678)

Mere listening does not make Satsanga, Good company means, establishing a link with Sat and giving Sat (truth) importance. (679)

To see in everybody the all-pervasive God is Satsanga. (the link with Sat). (680)

To have love for God, is also 'Satsanga'. Giving up attachment for the perishable, is also Satsanga. (681)

Just as food is essential to sustain a body, so is Satsanga. necessary, for spiritual life. (682)

Just as human form cannot be granted repeatedly,

so even on receiving human body, Satsanga is not repeatedly possible. (683)

Satsanga is not available easily by own efforts but only with the grace of God. (684)

Where there is selfishness, then it is not a Satsanga, but only its opposite. (685)

Under all circumstances, one learns the art of happiness only through Satsanga. (686)

To accept truth by itself, is Satsanga. (687)

Just as, if there is limited heat in the body, food is not digested, so if there is no inner desire, then the good ideas (Satsanga) are not imbibed. (688)

To obtain Satsanga is a sign of special divine grace. (689)

In business both gains and losses take place, but in good company or Satsanga there is only profit, never a loss. (690)

By giving importance to ideas at Satsanga, thoughts are purified and morbid feelings get destroyed. (691)

The more attachment is for sense pleasures, the more inertness arises in the intellect, by which even matters of essence read or heard in pious company, become incomprehensible. (692)

With the desire to gain something from the world, bad company begins. (693)

It is bad company, to accept one's relationship with the body and the world. (694)

Bad company in itself does not harm, but in accepting bad company, it becomes detrimental. (695)

Non-believers in God, the other world and righteousness (Dharma)—such an athiest's company would cause the worst downfall to man. (696)

Where there is inner weakness (faults) in a person, only then there is impact from external bad company. The reason is, that likes attract and unlikes do not. (697)

Pious company, good thoughts, holy scriptures and sorrow all four, are able to dissolve the linkage with the world, for a discerning person. (698)

If after practising and seeking for years, that Truth is not achieved, it is possible to realise it soon, by Satsaṅga . (699)

To practice devotion, is like earning wealth, and to be in pious company, is like being adopted by a person of wealth. Just as an adopted one succeeds to the adoptor's wealth, similarly by joining in spiritual meetings, even without practising devotion, dedication results. (700)

(XLIV) Time

Expended wealth could be retrieved, but lost time would not be regained. Time, like wealth, cannot be locked inside a safe. Therefore, always be careful and use time, in a good way. (701)

Money can be locked safely, but time could not be locked up. So do not waste your invaluable time in useless actions.   (702)

A person who does not use time beneficially, cannot be successful, in any field.   (703)

It appears as if time is passing, but in reality, it is the body that is going.   (704)

Ponder, that in the time that has passed, how much progress we might have made, by utilising that time, in the path of God-realisation.   (705)

(XLV) Aspirant

B y doing forbidden acts, nobody could be an aspirant.   (706)

If an aspirant desires, he could turn away from untruth, or come face to face with truth. He would have to choose either of these, then only, he would be able to save himself, from misfortune.   (707)

Firm determination that 'I am to realize God only' and to hold it fast is much essential for an aspirant.   (708)

An aspirant should not think of himself, as a seeker of pleasure or as a worldly person. He must always have the awareness, that he is an aspirant.   (709)

As much attachment with matter gets divorced,

so much that an aspirant acquires unusual quality, in him. (710)

An aspirant is, one who is constantly cautious. (711)

An aspirant must recognise his natural stay in God and what it is really. To accept one's existence, in the world, an aspirant fails in his efforts. (712)

An aspirant should consider, that if through him nobody is helped, nobody gains any benefit, nor is served in any way, what sort of an aspirant is he? (713)

In respect of his spiritual aspiration or fulfilment, he should not be worried, but his restlessness for attaining God should necessarily be there. The reason is that worry keeps one far from God and restlessness brings him closer to Him. (714)

Till the sense of individuality subsists an aspirant should not be complacent. (715)

To have difference of opinion with others, and to pattern your life according to your own faith, is not a fault. But to think ill of others' faith, or to refute it or to hate another's faith, is a defect. (716)

So long as an aspirant is not dissatisfied with his condition, he cannot make progress. (717)

An aspirant has only to be cautious about one matter. Should he see any perishable thing, he should not be caught by its attraction and give any importance to the same. He might make use of it, but not accept its subordination. (718)

An aspirant should not become a dogmatist, but only a seeker of the Truth. (719)

A pleasure seeker, loves sleep, like a friend, but a devotee and worshipper detests sleep, as an enemy. (720)

For a non-worshipper, the times were of Kaliyuga, while for a worshipper—devotee, these times are excellent. (721)

An aspirant should be ever vigilant—which means not to desire anything from anybody. (722)

An aspirant is one, who devotes himself, all the twenty-four hours. (723)

Whatever act is done—the smallest or the biggest—the aspirant must be careful, not to act it selfishly. (724)

An aspirant must always be vigilant to ensure, that nobody is hurt by any act of his. By hurting others, no peace could be had, even on undertaking worship for years. (725)

Whatever an aspirant knows, and recognising that much, should start making use of the same, and he would acquire further necessary knowledge, by himself. (726)

A body is of the world, and the self vests in God. So an aspirant should not accept himself as in the world, but would feel the existence of the self in God. (727)

An aspirant's decision on what should be done or not, he should leave it to the scriptures (Śāstras), and what should happen or not, be left to the will of God. (728)

Never consider yourself as a perfect man, but only as an aspirant. You could be deceived if you think of yourself as emancipated. (729)

An aspirant's job is not to rule, but to keep oneself under the rule of the seer of Truth and a well-wisher. (730)

An aspirant should ponder over it, that he does not want happiness, which is not eternal, and has pain associated with it. (731)

For an aspirant enjoying pleasure born of spiritual practice is especially an impediment, for him. (732)

The objective of an aspirant should not be to acquire learning, but to realize. By the knowledge acquired, he could become learned, an orator or a writer, but not a seer of Truth, liberated one while living, and a lover of God. (733)

If one looks to the beginning, he is not as aspirant, and one who notes the result, is an aspirant. (734)

To say 'I am an aspirant', if this is associated with vanity, then it is bad, but if it is in the spirit of duty, then it is helpful. It is vanity to say, that I am an aspirant while another person is not. And to say 'how could one work against spiritual discipline, that is spirit of duty or self-respect.   (735)

An aspirant should be a follower of truth, but not of any person, or sect etc.   (736)

(XLVI) Devotion

O nly repeating God's name (Japa) is not worship, but any God favourable act, and a feeling pulling one towards God, are also worship. (737)

The sole objective of attaining God and all acts pursuant, become the means, for the goal.   (738)

All actions for the world need to be done without getting attached with them, only treating these as a service or duty. But God's work (repetitive naming of God (Japa), meditation etc.) are absorbedly accomplished and treated as a special matter.   (739)

An aspirant should believe, with full faith in his heart that, "I belong to God and God is mine", then on his own he would naturally carry out his spiritual practice (Sādhana).   (740)

Day and night rapt practitioners of worship and meditation for God, benefit the world, more than those who merely act day and night.   (741)

What should a Guru be like?

Qualities— a saint, Guru and a great person must have:

1. One who, in our view, is truly knowledgeable and a knower of the Truth and excepting him there is no unusuality and speciality, noticeable in others.

2. One who knows the essence of Karmayoga, Jñānayoga, Bhaktiyoga and other means of realisation correctly.

3. One, in whose company or by whose words, all doubts in our mind, even without inquiring, are automatically removed.

4. In whose presence, happiness, and peacefulness are felt.

5. Who seems to maintain contact with us, only for the sake of our good.

6. Who expects nothing at all from us.

7. Whose all endeavours are devoted to the good of the aspirants.

8. In whose proximity, our desire for our goal increases by itself.

9. In whose company or by (vision) Darśana, discourses, memory etc., our defects and bad acts are removed and by itself we are blessed with good qualities and a behaviour of divine richness.

Pañcāmṛta

1. We are of God.

2. Wherever we live, it is in the court of God.

3. Whatever good we do, is that of God.

4. Whatever pure and Sāttvika eatables we partake is the offering of God.

5. With God's bestowed things, we serve only God's creation.

"I have only to realize God"—such determinate intellect is the root of all devotional action. But by treating the world as permanent, such intellect is not born. (742)

In being vain by the power of one's devotion, one gets anxious for his own shortcomings. (743)

By successfully accomplishing one's devotional practice, there remains no desire to live, no fear of death, no attachment for receiving things nor any allurement for doing something, these four are forever, eliminated. (744)

Whatever linkage and attraction man has with inert things, there is need to use all means for removing this attraction completely. (745)

Mere practice is not worship, but remembrance of God, and love for Him is worship. Without treating God as one's own, neither memory nor love awakens, for Him. (746)

Sādhana is made through the self, and not by mind, intellect and senses. (747)

All the means available for achieving God, should be given more respect, than God-realization itself. (748)

Sādhana if respected much it accelerates, if not so respected then it subsides and is not successful. (749)

All means to take one towards God, are

'Svadharma', (one's own duty), while acts that lead to the world, are Paradharma.   (750)

One who causes pain to others, he has no heart in his worship.   (751)

Whatever the conditions, one should engage oneself in spiritual practice. If one looks for satisfactory circumstances, then there might be no Sādhana, (no practice).   (752)

The essence of all means is, detachment from the world and to realise one's link with God.   (753)

Indifference towards the world and love for God, are the 'summum bonum' (ultimate good) of all means of devotion.   (754)

Whatever height one might reach by practice, one should never be satisfied with that state.   (755)

Whatever situation man faces, one should be happy with the same and that is worship.   (756)

While worshipping God, one should not remember the world, nor forget God, when acting in the world.   (757)

To meditate, to do penance or repeat God's name for one's self, is devilish, but it is human to do things for the good of others.   (758)

Just as good business means more money, so those devotional means are good, which attract your mind more to God.   (759)

Whatever means appear easy, start the same, and then what looks difficult becomes easier, and what is not understood, becomes comprehensible. (760)

One may take the assistance of any agent (such as body, mind) but one ought not to be dependent on it. This is known as 'Karaṇa Nirapekṣa' spiritual practice. (761)

Those who do not worship or practice devotion during childhood and youth, they would probably, not do so in old age. (762)

Sādhana is not like an everyday act, fixed for a designated time, but it has to be continuous. (763)

"I am not the body, but I am the master of the body". If this is well realised then all practices would become easy. (764)

Real practice is what is conducted continuously (every hour and each moment). Without continuous practice, we could not accomplish emancipation, in this life. (765)

If our remembrance of God is not automatic and have to be reminded then we must understand (Sādhana), that our practice has not really started yet. (766)

However much, we might practice, while maintaining the link with the world, there would be no realisation, in the present. (767)

By devotion, practice comes on its own. If there is no devotion practice has to be done. What comes by itself is natural and real, and what is compelled to be done, is fake. (768)

While doing work, God is forgotten only when one accepts the work as his own and doing it for oneself. (769)

In truth, practice is not action; actions and materials are at the forefront of 'Asādhana'. In practice, feelings and understanding are prominent. (770)

All practices lead to blessedness but a practice in which we have, liking, interest, faith and ability, that is best for us. (771)

(XLVII) Enjoyment of Pleasure and Hoarding

As the people's interest in pleasure and hoarding increases, so much does unrighteousness increase in society. With increase in irreligiousness in society, sinful conduct, strife, conflict and other faults increase, accordingly. (772)

Whatever pleasure you enjoy, ultimately distaste results—this is a rule. But man makes the mistake of not strengthening his feelings of distaste and makes these permanent. (773)

One who lives a life of pleasure, could not be

saved from pain, because pleasure arises from the relationship with the inert, and this inert link is the cause for the greatest pain of repeated birth and death.   (774)

In whatever pleasures, an ordinary person finds enjoyment, those pleasures, a thoughtful person considers as painful. Therefore, he neither enjoys these, nor becomes subservient to them.   (775)

Until the tendency to enjoy worldly pleasure is eliminated, howsomuch one might read and write, become clever and sensible, achieve much ability, become an orator, or writer of books, he would never get complete peace of mind.   (776)

Happiness derived from sense-objects, is neither ours nor is for us. Because, we are immortal and pleasure is ephemeral.   (777)

Increase in the pleasure—seeking and hoarding tendency, is the cause of famines.   (778)

Whatever thing, ability, power we have, all belong to the society and not to us. Our fault is, that we treat these things etc., as ours and use these for our gratification. By this, we helplessly suffer pain. (779)

Where one notices enjoyment of worldly pleasure, you must understand that there is danger around. (780)

Securing pleasure from a thing or a person, is sheer stupidity.   (781)

Worldly pleasures, to begin with appear sweet, but towards the end, these are like poison, always dangerous. (782)

Man can make use of given things by enjoying them and also serve others with these. His enjoyment leads him to a fall, but by serving others, he gets a rise. (783)

Enjoying pleasure with his own wish, makes a person to suffer unhappiness against his wishes. (784)

Using a thing for the good of others, is its good use, and to use it for personal pleasure, is its bad use. (785)

One who uses things, persons, circumstances and conditions etc., for personal pleasure, his uneasiness for achieving God does not awaken. (786)

So long as man keeps on receiving pleasure from the world, till then he would not be free from pain, whether he is a saint, a householder or whatever else. (787)

Whether one gets pleasure or not, if he is interested in worldly happiness, he is sure to have a fall. (788)

As much pleasure a man enjoys, he would so much become a slave of pleasure; and as a slave he would suffer pain. Therefore, it is necessary to give up the enjoyment of pleasure. (789)

One, whose intellect is much influenced by inert

things (worldly pleasures and hoarding), even if such a person might be highly educated, his fall is assured. But if his intellect does not attach importance to inertness and attaining God is his objective, such a person, even if not well-read, his ascent is sure to happen. (790)

If we receive happiness from anything, we must become its slave. An enjoyer of pleasure can never be independent. (791)

We are not to be enjoyers of pleasure, but we have to be givers of happiness. (792)

It might be 'Yoga' (spiritual union) or 'Bhoga' (enjoyment of pleasure) and if man receives happiness from either, he gets caught. (793)

(XLVIII) Pleasure and Pain

God does not care for pain arising from worldly things, and God cannot bear pain, coming from (real) pangs for the sake of God. (794)

Under God's auspicious dispensation, whatever favourable (pleasure giving) or unfavourable (painful) condition comes, it is only for our good. (795)

Being in pain or pleasure, is not the fruit of past acts, but a fruit of foolishness. This folly is wiped out by good company (Satsaṅga). (796)

Like an ever greedy person, an aspirant should

grant pleasure to others. By this, he would rise above pleasure and pain.   (797)

To make efforts to seek pleasure, is to invite pain, and to strive for others' happiness, is to invite bliss.   (798)

To get pain or pleasure, is the result of one's acts, but to become happy or sorry is the fruit of ignorance and foolishness. To avoid the fruit of action, is not possible by our hands, but eliminating foolishness is entirely within the grasp of a person.   (799)

When man serves others under happy circumstances, he does not become unhappy in painful conditions or does not desire pleasure for himself, then he is easily liberated from worldly ties.   (800)

Under the influence of nature-born pleasure, there is no end to the tradition of its succession.   (801)

In reality, happiness in favourable conditions is the reason for unhappiness under unfavourable circumstances; because a condition-bound pleasure seeker, cannot ever escape from unhappiness.   (802)

To give up the desire for happiness, unhappiness comes.   (803)

One who seeks happiness (for himself) from others, he would have to suffer great unhappiness.   (804)

We are ourselves the cause of our pain and none

else. So long as we treat others as cause of pain, till then our suffering would not be wiped out.   (805)

By being happy with one's own happiness, one surely becomes unhappy and acquiring happiness from other's happiness, his pain is lost forever.   (806)

To treat the body as 'I' and 'mine', is the cause of all pain.   (807)

So long as we draw happiness from the world, till then nature's link would not be lost.   (808)

The deficiency of a thing does not cause unhappiness, pain arises from the desire to get a thing.   (809)

Things do not cause unhappiness, as unhappiness is the result of the absence of proper thoughts, not of things. So by reflection pain is eliminated.   (810)

Happiness lies in stillness (giving up thoughts of the world) and not in enjoyment.   (811)

Wherever one notices worldly happiness, examine the same with deliberation, one would find unhappiness there, because the world, in reality, is unhappiness personified—'**Duḥkhālayam**' (Gītā VIII. 15).   (812)

If one wants to hear, pain is caused by not hearing. You want to see, and being not able to see, causes pain. Want power and you are unhappy with powerlessness; you want youth and one is sad for being old. It means that deficiencies themselves do not make people unhappy, but because of desire, and by the feeling of want, that people feel unhappy. (813)

If we are attached to the world, pain is endless. If we link ourselves with God, then happiness (bliss) is unlimited. (814)

Should you want happiness, then bring happiness to others. Just as you sow, so would you reap. (815)

When you notice worldly happiness around, be sure that there is some danger there. (816)

Everything is God—**'Vāsudevaḥ Sarvam'** (God is all) but He is not an object to be enjoyed. Anybody who wants to enjoy Him as object of enjoyment, suffers. (817)

In a household, if a feeling exists in all, that they should have happiness, then everybody would be unhappy. However if they feel as to how others would become happy, then every being would be happy. (818)

If you do not desire pain, do not seek worldly happiness. (819)

"Let others be happy". If this feeling prevails, then all would be happy including himself, who wishes so. "Let me be happy", if this feeling prevails, then all would be unhappy, as well as the person concerned. (820)

Why does worldly happiness not last ? As it is not at all, of us and for us. (821)

Happiness feels good, but its end is not good. Unhappiness makes one feel bad, but its result is good. (822)

A state of unhappiness in God's regime comes for our highest good. So one should not wish to remove it, and bear it peacefully. (823)

One who harms others, he in reality, harms himself most, and one who helps others to be happy, he verily makes himself happy. (824)

To be happy on receiving pain, is one of the highest means of Sādhana. (825)

Man is not free, to get rid of circumstances but he is quite free, capable and competent in not enjoying them or to be happy or sorrowful. It means that, in not being happy or unhappy, man is always free, capable and powerful. (826)

Until favourable or unfavourable circumstances influence till then, the Yogas of Karma, Jñāna and Bhakti or any other 'Yoga' are not successfully mastered. (827)

The world does not cause pain to anybody, but it is the acknowledged link with it, that inflicts pain. (828)

By worldly happiness, worldly unhappiness can

never be wiped out—this is a rule.   (829)

On gaining ingress to the world, greed increases and pain results. But on achieving God, love increases and bliss wells up.   (830)

A sufferer of pain can in future, be happy, but one who causes pain, can never be happy.   (831)

One who, in order to seek happiness, does not establish a tie up with anybody, he lives happily and dies happily. But those who link themselves with others, intent upon seeking something, they remain unhappy while alive and die in unhappiness, as well.   (832)

Just as thirst for water makes a person unhappy, though water by itself does not cause unhappiness. It is the attachment to the world happiness, that causes pain, while the world by itself does not cause unhappiness.   (833)

(XLIX) Service to Others (Welfare of Others)

I n doing harm to others, one harms himself and by doing good to others, he gains good—this is a rule.   (834)

Relations with the world are subject to and conditioned by obligations. There are ways to free oneself from these obligations, by serving all others and not desiring anything from anydody.   (835)

An aspirant may desire the realization of either

God with attributes or without attributes, he must, without fail, be devoted to the service and welfare of all beings. (836)

An aspirant lives in the world only for service to others, not for his own pleasure. (837)

An aspirant who serves God with a pure heart and in true faith, really serves all living beings, as God is the root of all. (838)

An aspirant must bear by himself all pains of his, howsoever great, but not tolerate the smallest pain that falls on others. (839)

By wishing to bring happiness to others, one loses his own desire for happiness to himself. (840)

That nobody should suffer no pain whatever, this feeling is a great worship. (841)

Just as a man goes to his office and only looks after his office work, so in this world also, only the work of the world has to be done, and nothing for himself. Then he easily delinks his attachment with the world and realizes the ever attained eternal God. (842)

Time, understanding, matter and effort—to consider using these four for oneself, is to misuse these. To employ these for the good of others, is their worthy and beneficial use. (843)

Whatever happiness one feels to derive from the

pleasures born of contact, and if such happiness one finds in giving pleasure to others, then there is no doubt, in one's blessedness (Kalyāṇa). (844)

Whatever happiness or comfort we have received, that is only for serving the world. (845)

Man's body has not been granted for enjoying ones pleasure, but only for service and bringing joy to others. (846)

God has granted such great privileges to man, that he could serve the living beings, humans, saints, Ṛṣis and great souls, the Devas, the manes, the spirits and all others. And not only that, but he could even serve The Almighty God. (847)

Without serving the world, the desire for action is not abandoned. (848)

Just as, by doing good work in a company, the owner becomes happy, so by our serving the world, its Master say God is pleased. (849)

As a mother's milk is not for herself but for a child, so whatever resources man has, are not for himself, but only for others. (850)

Just as, a sensual person has a lure for enjoyment, an obsessed person's weakness for his family, and a greedy person's love for wealth, so also a good person is devoted to the welfare of living beings. (851)

People are to be rendered service and beneficent

use of material things is to be made. (852)

By directing actions to the service of others, actions flow to the world, and an aspirant becomes free from the ties of action. (853)

One who always wants to feel oneness with all pervasive God, must necessarily be devoted to the welfare of living beings. (854)

Making use of gross, subtle and causal forms of body, in pilgrimage, fasting, charity, penance, reflection, meditation and Samādhi (trance) all good acts, in good faith selflessly done for others, become 'Svadharma' and these very acts done with personal motive become 'Paradharma'. (855)

The best use of a thing, is to use it for the good of others. (856)

A great man, is ever devoted to the good of others. (857)

Our life is not for ourselves, but for the good of others. (858)

The root of service, is to become unhappy with other's unhappiness. (859)

In doing good, we serve the society. Being free from wrong, humanity is served. Being free from desire, one serves oneself. In loving God, one serves God. (860)

One who takes the path of God whole heartedly,

through him good comes to others automatically. (861)

A thing given by the world, is solely for the service of the world, and not for anything else. (862)

Something may appeal to us, but it is not for our enjoyment, but only for service.   (863)

Man should do such things, that are good for him as well as, for the world, would be good now and also result in good.   (864)

If you serve your body, then you would be linked with the world. If you serve the world for the sake of God, then your relationship with God will strengthen.   (865)

One, who in his heart, feels good for all, he finds a place in the heart of God.   (866)

Spirituality has not deteriorated, but behaviour has, and must improve. Behaviour could improve by service to others discarding self-interest and vanity.   (867)

Whosoever, with feelings for the good of others, wherever he lives, would attain God there.   (868)

To turn towards God, we must turn away from the world. For turning away from the world, we must serve others, without thought of reward.   (869)

In service, to aspire for things, is a mistake. Whatever thing has been granted, the same should be rightly used, in serving.   (870)

In the world, as you do for others, the result would be the same for you, so always do good to others.   (871)

After abandoning selfishness and vanity, one who only applies himself to serving others, he truly lives.   (872)

Those who demand service, the present times are bad for them, but those who wish to serve others for them the times are propitious.   (873)

By any act of ours, nobody should suffer pain, howsoever little, this attitude is service.   (874)

By serving others unselfishly, not only does behaviour improve, but personal attachment would also be lost.   (875)

By serving family members, no delusion occurs. One deludes himself, only when one desires something from others.   (876)

After attaining God, man can benefit the world so much, that could not be compared with any charity or piety.   (877)

By serving a person, who bears enmity with us, we gain much, because in such a case there is no enjoyment of service.   (878)

Should an opportunity to render service arise, we should rejoice for that fateful chance.   (879)

If we keep our own good separate from that of the

entire creation, ego would continue, which is an obstacle for an aspirant. In other words, an aspirant's spiritual effort and his actions, should be directed towards the good of the world. (880)

(L) Nature

Selfishness and pride—both these spoil the nature of a person. An aspirant must always give up both selfishness and pride. (881)

Even after worship, meditation and spiritual efforts being done, presently, these may not show clear benefits, because of impurity of human nature and behaviour. So every aspirant must make special efforts to improve his nature. (882)

There is no better progress than purifying one's nature. (883)

Of him whose nature improves, for him world betters. (884)

One whose nature is to cause pain to others, he not only suffers pain himself, but also makes others suffer. However, if one's nature is to give pleasure to others, he not only gives pleasure to them, but he himself also gains pleasure. (885)

Man can improve his nature by himself, others can only suggest remedies and assist him. (886)

Our nature can improve, when we do justice to ourselves, meaning that we are punitive to ourselves and compassionate with others.   (887)

Good company, good scriptures and good thoughts—these three improve our nature.   (888)

One whose nature improves, he does not face a downfall.   (889)

"Shall do later", is a means leading to a great fall. It is difficult for a person of that nature to receive blessedness (Kalyāṇa).   (890)

(LI) Self

An aspirant should not watch the ever-changing conditions, but direct his attention to the non-changeable entity (Self).   (891)

The self is desireless. Selfishness arises from a link with matter.   (892)

The body and other material things are ever-changing. One who perceives thus, never changes. That is why no change is ever noticed in the Self.   (893)

The being, in reality, is free from the sense of doership and devoid of pleasure and pain. But due to error it regards itself as the doer and associating itself with the fruits of actions it becomes happy or unhappy.   (894)

Only due to our association with actions and material things, we do not have Self-realization. (895)

Our body exists in the world, but ourself (self) is

vested in God.   (896)

The self is Pure Existence not ego. Giving up ego, realise the natural stay of the Self in Pure Existence.   (897)

We ourselves are the 'Self' not different from it. If it is difficult to know it, what could be easy? (898)

Our Existence is not subordinated to a thing, person or action.   (899)

The Self is 'Pure Existence', 'Pure Being'. To mix anything with it is ignorance and bondage.   (900)

The self is not subordinate to the body, but the body is subordinate to the self. It means that self without body can remain, but our body could not live without the self.   (901)

(LII) Miscellaneous

W ithin an aspirant, every time he should have a feeling that one is not a resident here, but (being a fraction of God) he resides in God's abode.   (902)

In one's earning, not an iota of anybody's claim should be included and one should be most careful about the same.   (903)

When the sentient identifies itself with the inert, then finiteness appears or ego arises. From the ego emerges mineness, which leads to morbid feelings. From mineness arises desire, which results in absence of peace (Śānti). (904)

An aspirant should so believe that, whatever he does is the worship of God and whatever is happening, is God's sport. (905)

At the present, man is degrading himself to worse than animals. Animals make use of things they need to maintain themselves with and do not take away the rights of others, but man after depriving others of their rights, hoards things. (906)

To fulfil the bodily needs of a person, God makes arrangements, but no means exist to satisfy his greed. (907)

When an aspirant sees his faults as faults, he becomes unhappy with them. When the existence of these defects becomes unbearable for him, then these do not continue. God's grace soon destroys these faults. (908)

The mind remembers better than the eyes. Even more than the mind, the intellect remembers still better. And better still than the intellect, perceives the self. If the self catches something, it remembers it ever and for all the time. (909)

In one's place or sphere, those persons who are considered pre-eminent whether as teachers, lecturers, preceptors, masters, leaders, administrators, chief monks, story narrators, priests and others, they have to be very careful specially about their conduct, by which they would bring to bear good influence on other people.　　(910)

If you want to do something, then serve others. You want to know something, then know the self. You want to believe in something, then believe in God. All these three steps would result, in the same thing. (911)

If a pen is good, then writing can be good, but that does not make one a better writer. So, if there is purity of inner faculty, then actions can be pure, but the actual doer, does not become pure.　　(912)

People may think highly good of us, while we are not so good, and others may think of us as bad, but we are worse than that. After realising this truth, we should give up the desire that "others may think of us as good" but in our own view, we should endeavour to become better and better.　　(913)

The desire for the pleasure born of sense-contacts is more deadly than happiness itself. The desire for the body to continue is more fatal than having a body. The delusion towards a family, is more ruinous than having a family. The greed of wealth, is more destructive than wealth itself.　　(914)

The world you perceive is not to be accepted as yours, but to render service to it, and who cannot be seen, that God must be acknowledged as yours and remembered.　　(915)

Do not abuse the world granted to you, do not disrespect the known essence and do not show lack of faith in God, duly believed. (916)

In our hearts, the inert (body-world) has claimed more respect and so much more disrespect has been shown to God. That disrespect would eventuate in our fall and degradation. (917)

The intellect granting importance to perishable materials, cause a downfall of man, while intellect established in glory of God raises him high. (918)

One who misuses a thing, person etc., he is deprived of these and suffers unhappiness by their loss. (919)

Whosoever is one's own, is always our own, and what was not one's own, at any time, that can never be our own. (920)

What belongs to all, is also our own. What is not owned by anybody at any time, could at no time be our own. (921)

Whatever thing or person attracts an aspirant, then he should think of God in them. (922)

To perceive God uniformly at all places, is an equable view of Him. Watching material nature and (body-world) oriented panorama is a contrary view of Him. (923)

Man should himself not resolve on anything, but

he should have no separate wish from that of God, meaning that he should be most happy in the dispensation of God.   (924)

Every man should be cautious always, that he is not causing any difficulty or loss to anybody. (925)

Make it a rule, that if anybody does not fulfil our wish at any time, then we shall not be annoyed. (926)

God is the master of the world and to believe that I am the master of my body, is a mistake. One, who is the master of the world, is also the master of a body.   (927)

Like a child, under all circumstances calls for his mother, so should a person, under any condition invoke God.   (928)

For a just person, there is peace of mind in acting justly, and unjust action invites loss of peace of mind, for an unjust man.   (929)

Whatever causes harm to oneself and others, presently or ultimately, all such acts are 'Asat' (not good).   (930)

In the world, whatever things you have a right to and are available, these things also would not remain with you. Then, what you are neither entitled to nor become available, why hope for these?   (931)

If you must know something, then realise the eternal, what use knowing the perishable?   (932)

Think over it: 'What is good for us and what we can do and do we accomplish that? (933)

To think of the one going, as on the way out, and the one who stays as come to stay—this is appropriate understanding. (934)

We should not do anything wrongly, that we could never straighten later. (935)

Every circumstance is the sport of God, and enjoy it by watching the same. (936)

Duality and non-duality are simply concepts. The Tattva is, neither dual nor non-dual. (937)

If we have committed no crime, and our actions are correct, then we should not fear anything. If one is afraid, then something or the other is wrong and somewhere or the other, we have made a mistake. It also means that we do not have firm faith in our own innocence. (938)

Before starting any act, we must ask ourselves, as to why we are doing such a thing. (939)

Right or wrong lies in our view. In the eyes of God, everything is alright and nothing goes wrong. (940)

If others see good qualities in us, that shows their goodness and magnanimity, but for us to acknowledge the qualities as ours, is the misuse of their goodness and magnanimity. (941)

The best way to gain education is to, abide by the master's instructions and to please him. What education we acquire by pleasing of our master, cannot come by our own efforts.   (942)

What work gets done by exclaiming for God, could not be accomplished by mere understanding and thinking.   (943)

The unhappiness of not attaining God, is many thousand times greater, than worldly happiness. (944)

Just as a physician prescribes or gives a medicine, in that lies our good. So whatever God dispenses, therein lies the greatest good for us.   (945)

Just as ghee held in the body of a cow, is not useful, so mere learning is not of much use.   (946)

"I am the knower" or "I am not knower", these both are admissions of the ignorant.   (947)

True beauty lies in the character of a person. (948)

To remember something, remember God, and to think of work, serve others.   (949)

To admit the truth, is man's bounden duty. (950)

If each person, one by one reforms himself, then the whole society would be reformed.   (951)

Should you want happiness from your children, then give happiness to your parents and serve them.   (952)

To wish ill of others, is to invite ill to oneself.   (953)

Remember—all dispensations of God are for your greatest good. (954)

By relating anything about yourself appearing special to you, in reality it is your subordination of that. (955)

In the end, one has to go alone. So from the beginning one should get lonely, by giving up the attachment of things, persons and actions. (956)

It is an all important rule to follow: to always remember God, and an over-riding abstention to give up desire. (957)

Contentment, is the basic Mantra for reforming society. (958)

"Unity in diversity" and "Diversity in unity", is a special feature of Hindu religion. (959)

A person taking refuge in untruth, cannot harm us. (960)

There is nothing so invaluable in the world, as devotion to God. (961)

Efforts to change the conditions are fruitless, and efforts to make good use of the conditions are useful. (962)

As man creates more needs, he would as much become more subservient. (963)

It is most surprising that things granted by God appeal to man, but not God Himself. (964)

Whether people accept us as good or not, know us as good or not, think of us as good or not, but if our feelings are good, then all the time our mind would be happy and on death there would be salvation. (965)

If a bad thought arises, be careful that if death should take place suddenly, what would happen then? If one always thinks of God and death took place at any time, then there is no worry. (966)

By the deterioration of personal life, the whole society is affected and by improvement of personal life, society improves, as people make a society. (967)

In the separation of God, the pain that results, gives much more happiness, than from worldly happiness. (968)

If one is in fear of God, scripture, Gurujana and the world, he in reality becomes fearless. (969)

We separate from the one that is ever separate, and we shall get, what is ever got. (970)

In receiving a thing, with the pleasure of another, is like getting milk. Having a thing by request is like obtaining water, while getting something after causing pain to others, is like having blood. (971)

Don't indulge in worry and remorse and be careful for the future, so that you do not repeat the same. (972)

A thing that erases, cannot stay for even a moment. (973)

To notice something special in oneself, can be seen only by one's pride. (974)

We can live without material things, and what we can live without, why should we become slaves of these? (975)

The body seems near and yet God appears far off—that is ignorance. The reason is, that the body is always unattained (as it is decaying), while God is ever attained. With a body there is not even a minute's union, while with God there could not be a moment's separation. (976)

To believe the body as separate from the world and the self from God, is a mistake. (977)

A truly righteous person has no need or interest in anybody. But the world has need for such a one. (978)

If man shows disrespect for his discrimination, then his discrimination hides. However, if he respects his discrimination, then it multiplies, to the extent that he can reach God, even without a scripture or Guru. (979)

When we do not accept everybody's words, so if others also do not listen to us, then we should not be annoyed. (980)

If there is no greed within, then needed things would come, on their own. It is greed that becomes an impediment in achieving things.   (981)

One should not show any disrespect to any person. In reality it would tantamount to disrespecting his own self, as the whole world is God itself.   (982)

Having been born in India and a man not attracted by God, is a matter for surprise and distress, as birth in India is for salvation and even Devas desire to be born here.   (983)

Dharma (virtue) is rooted in the renunciation of selfishness and in doing the good of others.   (984)

To follow the tenets of one's Dharma (religion) himself there is no better exhortation for Dharma.   (985)

"Bless me"—By not seeking blessings, become eligible for them.   (986)

The present needs to be reformed, then the past and the future both, would automatically be reformed.   (987)

It is an unhappy person, who makes others unhappy. It is the subservient person, who wants to subordinate others.   (988)

An ignorant person takes the past as a dream, while a knowledgeable one, takes the present like a dream.   (989)

By itself, importance of a thing is nil and it depends on its good use. (990)

Feeling for the need of God, is prayer. (991)

Greed for an unreal thing, is a barrier to achieving the same, but the craving for truth, accelerates achieving the truth. (992)

In maintaining our body, every care should be taken, that the least time and expense are incurred. (993)

The subordination to nature's matter (par) makes one subject to others and the slave of pleasure, thus a greater slave. The subordination of self (Svarūpa) is independence and subordination of one's own God— means greater independence. (994)

Watching TV or seeing movies, harms people in four ways; (1) damage to character, (2) waste of time, (3) loss of eye-sight, and (4) loss of money. (995)

By doing something one establishes oneself in nature, while by doing nothing, we are vested in God. (996)

Just as steady water allows impurities to settle down, similarly speech, mind and intellect, on silence (by peace and non-action), all morbid feelings are eliminated, ego is dissolved and realisation of the self takes place. (997)

Those who are themselves not good, and not used

to doing good, they feel that the times are not auspicious to do good, presently.   (998)

So long as man, compared with others sees something special in himself, he could be an aspirant, but not an emancipated soul.   (999)

God is attained one and the world is an apparition. What we could gain is invisible, that is called— 'Prāpta' or obtained one. What we see, but is not attained is called, 'Pratīti' i.e., apparition.   (1000)